The Cathar

A Megalithic Journey into the Histories and Mysteries of the Languedoc

The Cathars, Rennes-le-Château, Knights Templar,
The Nazi Connection, Sacred Geometry,
The Priory of Sion

To Nigel & Barbara with fond memories of the tour of 2010

Neil

Neil McDonald BA(Hons)
Megalithic Publishing
2010

The Cathar Country

First Published by Megalithic Publishing 2010

© 2010 Neil McDonald

The rights of Neil McDonald to be identified as author of this work has been asserted in accordance with the Copyright, Design and Patents Act 1988

All rights reserved. No part of this book may be reproduced, stored in or introduced into a retrieval system, or transmitted, in any form or by any other means (electronic, mechanical, photocopying, recording or otherwise) without the written permission of the publisher.

Any person who does any unauthorized act in relation to this publication may be liable to criminal prosecution and civil claims for damages. The book is sold subject to the condition that it shall not, by the way of trade or otherwise, be lent, re-sold, hired out or otherwise circulated, without the publisher's prior concent, in any form or binding cover other than in which it is published, and without similar conditions, including this condition being imposed on the subsequent publications.

ISBN- 978-1-4461-2327-0

www.megalithictours.com

The Cathar Country

The Cathars
Little foxes in the Vineyard of the Lord

Take us the foxes, the little foxes, that spoil the
vines: for our vines [have] tender grape
Song of Solomon 2:15

Contents

Introduction	8
Chapter 1.	
History of the Languedoc	10
Early Languedoc	11
Magdalenien period 15,000-9,000BC	11
Neolithic 4,500BC	11
The first millennium, the Druids, the Tectosages, the Romans and the Visigoths	12
The Merovingians	13
The Saracens	16
The Carolingians	16
Chapter 2.	
The Legend of Mount Cardou	20
Chapter 3.	
The Cathars	25
The Gnostic-Dualistic Christians	25
Gnosticism	25
Dualism	29
The fate of the Cathars – The Albigensian Crusade	32
Beziers	37
Carcassonne	39
Simon de Montfort	42
Toulouse	47
The Inquisition	55
Montsegur	57
The last days of the Cathars	64

Chapter 4.
François Bérenger Saunière and Rennes-le-Château   70

François Bérenger Saunière   73
    Sauniere's Astrology   75
    The Profile   76
Background to the mystery   78
The mystery unfolds   86
    The Pillars   86
    The Parchments   89
    Discovered a Tomb – Rain in the Afternoon   95
    Interpretation of the Headstone   100
    Interpretation of the Gravestone   101
The Prosperous Priest   102
The Church of St. Mary Magdalene   107
    The Entrance tympanum   108
    Devil and Angels   112
    A fresco of Jesus, the Sals valley
    and a Bas-reliefs of Mary   121
    The Church Statues   127
    Stations of the Cross   130
    A Hidden Room   133
Conflict with the Bishop   135
The fairytale in decline   138
The mystery goes on   144

Chapter 5.
January 17th, Priests, Players and Post Mortems   145
17th January   145
The Abby Bérenger Sauniere – Rennes-le-Château   148
The Abby Henry Boudet – Rennes-Les-Bains   149
The Abby Antoine Gelis – Causaussa   151
Noel Corbu, Henri Buthion and Jean-Luc Robin
the Keepers of the Domain   153

Chapter 6.
The mystery of the 'Two Towers'   156
The British Tower   163
Katharine Maltwood   164

Chapter 7.
The Emerald Temple of Rennes   166
The Temple of Venus, Isis and the Magdalene   166
A hexagram of churches   170
Wood's Genisis   172

Chapter 8.
The Knights Templar, the true Knights of the Grail   176
Formation of the Templars – The orthodox account   177
Bernard of Clairvaux   179
Hugh I, the Count of Champagne   180
The Council of Troyes   181
The Rex Deus Families   183
The Temple Mount Timeline   185
The Foundation of the Brotherhood   187
The growth of the Order   191
Friday 13th and the End-Game   196
The Swiss Banking Connection   200
The Bruce and Bannockburn   202

Chapter 9.
The Priory of Sion — **204**
The New Priory — 205
An Ancient Order — 210
A Continuing Order? — 213
Into the future — 215

Chapter 10.
The Nazis, 'Indiana Jones' and the Temple of Solomon — **217**

Bibliography — **230**

The Cathar Country

Introduction

You are about to embark on a journey to lands steeped in mystery and legend. To lands known since Old Testament times to be of great spiritual importance and to lands with a rich, diverse and fascinating history. Our journey begins at the dawning of time and runs right up to the present day.

These beautiful lands in Southern France's Languedoc and Aude Valley have been the home to the mighty Visigoths. They were the natural homeland of the Knights Templar and they were the homeland of the dualistic Christian sect of Catharism. More recently they were the home of Francois Bérenger Sauniere, the priest of the tiny hill top hamlet of Rennes-le- Château, who's intriguing story inspired a BBC documentary series in 1972, which was followed by the World best seller, Holy Blood and Holy Grail in 1982 and then in 2003, Dan Brown's international block-buster novel 'The Da Vinci Code', which in turn became a massively successful Hollywood Movie.

The Cathar Country has been inhabited since before recorded history and as the millennia have passed it has been a centre of peace and tolerance when allowed to run its own affairs, times which produced advancements in society leading to near renaissance. But these lands have also been witness to the most brutal side of mankind's nature when outside interests viewed the freedoms developing in the Languedoc as evil and contra to their own religious belief systems. The orthodox Roman Catholic Church set about a mission of genocide the likes of which Europe had never witnessed and which resulted in the massacre of thousands.

The Cathar Country

In the following pages we will look at these happenings and at the Cathars. We will also look at more recent times and the mysteries which this area seems to produce. This work is presented in order to provide a sound background for people interested in this area of France. It will also be of interstest, to those seeking an honest and fresh look at the history of the area ++and in particular anyone preparing to visit and looking for a concise coverage of the history and mysteries of the Languedoc.

Chapter 1.

History of the Languedoc

The Cathar Country lies in the South of France, just over the Spanish boarder on the vast fertile plains between the foothills of the Pyrenees and the shores of the Mediterranean.

Map showing the position of the Languedoc

The history of the Languedoc is long and varied with evidence of human occupation amazingly as early as 15,000 BC. The region has seen times of peace and tolerance contrasted with long periods of some of the most brutal warring known to Europe, brought here by religious zealotism and compounded by the greed of so called great men with an eye on these fertile lands.

Early Languedoc

The Magdalenien Period
(15,000 – 9,000BC)

There can be no better example of just how long these lands have been occupied than the amazing prehistoric cave paintings of Niaux dating back to the Magdalenian period up to 17,000 years ago. The caves are one of an assortment to be found in the foothills of the Pyrenees and are located not far south of the town of Foix.

The 'Hall of the Black Bison', where the cave paintings are found, is a good few hundred yards into the mountain. Today we have the benefit of electric lights but how did the ancestors keep these places lit and why did they choose such an isolated place for these apparently sacred paintings. These Bison and Gazelles are painted with real sophistication, they really knew their art. When visiting the caves you get the distinct impression of a civilised people expressing a wonder of their surroundings

Neolithic Languedoc
(Around 4,500BC)

There is plenty of evidence of early settlement around Carcossonne and Renne from the Neolithic period around 4,500BC, when the South of France warmed up and went through its period of agricultural settlement. Around this time known as the 'Agricultural Revolution', which happened around 1,000 years earlier than it did in Britain, the ancestors began to build huge megalithic structures. There are many ancient sites scattered around the Cathar Country such as Dolman/Chambered Tombs and the 'Le Grand Menhir', the tallest monolith in Southern France. These early stone sites provide evidence of a much earlier belief system than that of the Cathars, but the question has to be whether there is in fact any connection between the mysteries of the ancestors and the latter day mystery schools, which may well have influenced the Cathars.

The First Millennium
The Druids, the Tectosages, the Romans (122BC-410AD) and the Visigoths (410-508AD)

Until the Romans invaded around 122BC, taking control of the Narbonnais area and settling in Carcassonne, the Languedoc was inhabited by an indigenous people. There was also a Druidic priestly race called the Tectosages who lived in the area and enjoyed elevated status as esoteric teachers. The name Druid comes from the Irish 'those who know', suggesting the notion that these sages were the custodians of ancient teachings. These mysteries are said to have been passed down since the beginnings of mankind and to have gone through the hands of the mystery schools, down the ages and at one time to have heavily contributed to the teachings of the Cathars.

The area was part of the Roman Empire until the Visigoths, one of the spreading Germanic tribes of the time, plundered Rome in 410AD. They proceeded to build a huge empire with Toulouse as its capital. They also created the mighty city of Rhedae a place which is central to our story because today it has reduced from a city of more than 30,000 people, equal in size to Carcassonne, to the tiny hill top village of Rennes-le-Château.

The Merovingians
'The Long Haired Sorcerer Kings'
(508-725AD)

*He shall separate himself from wine and song..........
All the days of the vow of his separation there shall no razor come upon his head: until the days be fulfilled, in the which separates himself unto the Lord, he shall let the locks of his hair of his head grow... And this is the law of the Nazarite.*
Numbers 6:3 5-13

The beginnings of the 6th century are known today as the Dark Ages, a time which coincides with not only the earliest Grail stories, but with the era of King Arthur. It is also at this time that we encounter the Merovingians, another Germanic race. These 'Long Haired Sorcerer Kings' were ruled by a long royal line whose ancestry is said to go back to Noah, through the Nazarite tradition. They were said to have had supernatural powers, closely associated with their long hair. Samson and Samuel are recorded as being of this bloodline.

The position of Chief Nazarite was traditionally held by a member of the line of David. Although the Merovingians were of this bloodline, they were not practicing Jews and followed a Gnostic initiatory path more akin to the Druids and other Nazarite sects, such as the Essenes. They were well known as esoteric teachers, judges, faith healers and clairvoyants.

One of the abiding symbols of the Merovingians was the bee and hundreds of pure gold bees were found in King Childeric's tomb. This custom, which goes back at least to ancient Egypt and probably before, endured through the centuries and when Napoleon was crowned Emperor in 1804, he made sure that golden bees were attached to his coronation robes. Modern day mystery schools continue this tradition and the 'Servants of the Light' for example; have the bee as the centre piece of their symbol of the first degree of initiation. Amongst other things this indicates the multiple hive mind working to a common purpose.

In 508 the armies of the Meroviginian king Clovis took Toulouse from the Visigoths, forcing them south to Carcassonne. Whilst retreating the Visigoths moved all their treasure to Rhedae, where they created a 'Fort-Knox', type stronghold. For some reason the Meroviginians didn't force their advantage any further and thus kept the lands of the Languedoc, then known as Septimania, intact. Could this be because these lands were held to be special in some way, if not sacred to these priest kings, with such a long lineage going back through King David?

One member of the Meroviginian line is of particular interest to our story and that is King Dagobert II, whose story reads like a fairy tale and forms a continuing part of our story.

When Dagobert's father, Sigebert II died in 656, Dagobert was kidnapped by Grimoald, the Mayor of the palace, who engineered his own son to the throne. Dagobert was secretly exiled to Ireland, where he was put under the supervision of the monks of Slane monastery. Here he was educated to a higher level than he could have ever received in the lands of the Franks, or France as we now know it. He is also known to have attended the court of the High Kings of Tara. In 666 he married Mathilda, a Celtic princess and moved to York and became close friends with Saint Wilfrid, the bishop of York.

When Mathilda died in 670, the influential Christian dignitary Saint Wilfrid, saw his opportunity to move and to show his true colours. He sought a new match for Dagobert, which would fulfil the goal of the Church of Rome, to unify all of France under its power.

Wilfrid could not have found a better suitor for his cause and in 671 Dangobert II married Giselle de Razes, daughter of the count of Razes (or Rennes-le-Château) and niece of the king of the Visigoths. If Dagobert was to regain his rightful throne, this marriage would have united the Merovingians bloodline with the royal bloodline of the Catholoic Visigoths and thus would have brought a vast empire firmly under control of the Roman Church.

Unfortunately for Wilfrid and Rome, Dagobert was his own man and following his reinstatement to the throne he set about strengthening his own authority. He moved to live at Rennes-le- Château, where he amasses a huge treasure trove which was to be used for the re-conquest of Aquitaine. He had also fought hard to reduce the power of Rome in his lands and as so had gained powerful enemies.

His death came on a hunting expedition which appeared to have a ritual element. It was the year 679 when, on 23rd December around the winter solstice, he went out hunting in the sacred forest of Woëvre. He sat down near a spring;

runnuing near to a large oak, to take some rest and one of the servants struck the king whilst he was praying.

But that is by no means the last we hear of Dagobert or the Merovingians; in fact they are immersed in the story of Renne-les-Château. Dagobert came to life again in 1891, when Bérenger Saunière is said to have found a coded message in a parchment, whilst renovating the church at Rennes.

The Saracens
(725-759AD)

Trouble for the Merovingians began with the growth of the new religion of Islam. After the death of Mohammed in March 632 Islam was borne and within 5 years they had conquered Jerusalem. The Muslim Saracen armies continued to expand their empire and in 718 their ships passed through the Straight of Gibraltar and by 725 they had conquered Visigothic Spain and finally the Languedoc.

The Carolingians
(759-840AD)

The job of halting the expansion of the Saracen, Muslim armies fell to Charles (the Hammer) Martel (688-741) who won the Battle of Tours (also known as the Battle of Poitiers) in 732. Charles's victory has often been regarded as decisive for world history, since it preserved western Europe from Muslim conquest and Islamization.

In the mean time an ongoing power struggle was taking place in the Merovingian courts, between the royal bloodline and the 'Mayors of the Palace', who were increasingly building their power base. In 759 Pepin the Short (714-768), the son of Charles Martel and the father of Charlemagne, who was the presiding Mayor of the time, drove the Saracens out of Septimania and back over the Pyrénées. Pepin is considered to be the first real Carolingian king and as time went on marriages between the Merovingian and the Carolingians confirmed their status as rightful kings.

It is of interest to note that according to the work of Tim Wallace-Murphy, it is the Carolingians who could claim the rightful bloodline connection to the line of David. Or could it be that this connection was made by marriage into the Merovingian household?

On the death of Pepin, the crown of the Franks was passed to his son Charles, who would soon be known as Charles the Great, or Charlemagne as we know him today. As a staunch Catholic Charlemagne was more than prepared to protect Rome and when Pope Hadrian I came under attack from Lombard invaders he sent a defending army.

Following this he set out on a 30 year campaign to subdue and convert the people of Saxony in the Rhine Valley and beyond, to the Catholic faith heavily backed by the threat of the sword.

For service to the Roman Church, Charlemagne was proclaimed 'Holy Roman Emperor', which resulted in Rome now becoming the seat of a vast empire covering the whole of Western Europe, whose rulers had become in reality vassals of the Pope and were now answerable to Rome.

Charlemagne died at the age of 72 after reigning for 47 years. His successor was 'Louis the Pious', his only surviving son. Emperor Louis I (814-840), was the last to rule over the great empire, as he divided his lands between his two sons, thus creating roughly what we know today as France and Germany.

At the same time authority over the southern lands of the Languedoc diminished as the inhabitants had only ever paid lip service to their conquerors. They took the opportunity to reassert their independence and the great Languedoc families of Trencavel, Toulouse and Foix emerged as popular leaders.

Nostadamus House, Alet-les-Bains

The Cathar Country

Under these leading families there followed a time of peace, prosperity and religious tolerance. The region became a fertile environment for philosophy, literature, politics, science, art and religious thought of all kind. The Jewish community, which had settled in Narbonne, began to thrive throughout the area without persecution. In Alet-les-Bains Nostadamus was known to have studied and outwardly discussed esoteric philosophy.

With freedom comes advancement and human evolution and it is highly probable that if things were allowed to take their course, the renaissance would have taken hold here, instead of 200 years later in Italy.

Chapter 2

The Legend of Mount Cardou

Mount Cardou

One of the most fascinating legends associated with this region, is the one least spoken of, yet one which appears to be at the centre of all the others, the 'Legend of Mount Cardou'. The majestic massive of Cardou can be seen standing out as the tallest mountain in the area. It is known locally as a holy mountain and local fork-lore tells of catacombs running through it and of a secret hidden chamber holding the remains of ancient kings.

The Cathar Country

Now this leads to the hub of the matter and that is Cardou's connection to the story of the flood deluge, which is not only told in the Bible but also in many other traditions throughout the World. For example in the Greek tradition Pyrrha and Deucalion were the only survivors of the flood and a connection has been made between the name Pyrrha and the Pyrenees and thus the area which includes Mount Cardou. It is said that the Flood goddess or the person her character is based upon may have been buried beneath one of these mountains.

In fact in several traditions, the place where the Ark came to rest is called "Kardo" and a particular example is 'The Book of the Cave of Treasures' an ancient Syrian text which was written down as early as the mid 300sAD and which records a verbal tradition from thousands of years earlier.

The text was translated by Sir Wallis Budge (1857-1934), a Cornishman from Bodmin who was a world renowned Egyptologist, Orientalist, and philologist. He worked for the British Museum and published numerous works on the ancient Near-East and was responsible for translating many ancient manuscripts, including the Egyptian 'Book of the Dead'.

The 'Book of the Cave of Treasures' tells of the history of the Earth from creation right through to the crucifixion. It tells of how the Ark of the flood came to rest on Mount Kardo after 150 days and that from here mankind spread out again around the planet. According to the text, a chamber beneath the mountain called the 'Cave of Treasure' holds the Biblical fathers of mankind, together with the secrets of mankind itself.

Jewish Rabbinic lore says that when a patriarch dies, his family transports his body to the Cave of Treasures. There he is buried alongside his ancestors in a secret tomb that is also a repository for sacred treasures, including the most ancient 'secrets of the Church'.

In the 'Book of the Cave of Treasures' God speaks to Adam saying;

'command thy sons, and order them to embalm thy body after thy death with myrrh and cassi. And they shall place thee in this cave..... in the centre of the earth....'Adam took from the skirts of the mountain of Paradise, gold, myrrh, and frankincense, and he placed them in the cave, and consecrated it that it might be the house of prayer for him and his sons. And he called it 'The Cave of Treasures.' (Budge, Sir E. A. Wallis, KT, *The Book of the Cave of Treasures*)

So according to the evidence 'The Cave of Treasures' lies hidden in Mount Cardou. It holds the bodies of the Fathers of mankind, together with the history of mankind itself and it lies in the centre of the World. So where is the centre of the world? Ignatius Donnelly wrote;

'The Romans and the Persians called the line of the axis of the globe Cardo, and it was to Cardo the needle pointed. Now 'Cardo was the name of the mountain on which the human race took refuge from the Deluge... the primitive geographic point for the countries which were the cradle of the human race.' (Donnelly, Ignatius, *Atlantis, the Antediluvian World*)

It is from this that we get our word 'cardinal', as in the cardinal points and probably the title given to a church rank in orthodox Christianity. Further to this the original primal meridian, before it was moved to Greenwich, the so called 'The Rose Line' actually centres on Mt Cardou.

Château de Arques

This strange story may be difficult to accept, but the mystery is only compounded by the name of the village of 'Arque', which lies at the foot of the mountain of Cardou. Medieval castles were usually used as places of safety and refuge for nearby inhabitants of the villages and towns in times of danger. The positioning of Arque's castle however is another anomaly as it is not situated anywhere near the town and lies on the outskirts, as if to defend some unknown treasure. The Knights Templar seemed also to have believed the story and organised a huge engineering project on the mountain, which involved extensive smelting, suggesting that they were not only on an exercise of discovery but also of concealment. There is great evidence that Saunière, the infamous priest of Rennes-le-Château and his counterpart Boudet, also believed it as they are recorded to have walked extensively on the mountain and to have carried many rocks back to the church.

Chapter 3

The Cathars

The Gnostic-Dualistic Christians

Although an awful lot has been written and spoken about the Cathars, their background and beliefs still appear to be shrouded in misunderstanding and misinformation. Just exactly who were they, what did they believe and what happened to them?

The religious stand point of the Cathars is probably best described as Gnostic, Dualistic Christianity. This differed in many respects to that of the Roman church and so is regarded by them as a heresy, but their belief system stems from an ancient tradition going back thousands of years and into time immemorial.

Gnosticism

"Know thyself"
Thales (635 BC - 543 BC)

"He who knows others is learned;
He who knows himself is wise."
Lao-tzu (6th Century BC)

The Cathar Country

*"Wherever we go, whatever we do,
self is the sole subject we study and learn."*
Ralph Waldo Emerson (1803-1882)

The theologian and theosophist GRS Mead said that there are four World religions. These are in reverse chronological order;

1. **Islam** – founded by the profit Mohammed, who was born around 570AD in the city of Mecca
2. **Christianity** – in its present form was founded at the Council of Nicea in what is present day Turkey in 325AD, by the Roman Emperor Constantine I under the Nicene Creed.
3. Buddhism - Buddha Shakyamuni, the founder of earthly Buddhism, was born as a prince in 624 BC in a place called Lumbini, which was originally in northern India but is now part of Nepal
4. **Gnosticism** – is probably the oldest belief system in the world encompassing such religions as:
    Zoroastrianism – possibly pre-6000BC
    Manichaeism
    Sol Invictus
    The early Egyptian religions
    Mithraism
    The Mysteries of Euclid
    Early Christianity
        The Nazerites
        The Essenes
    Hinduism
    Druidism
    Bogomillism
    Catharism

The Cathar Country

The Megalithic religion. Chambered Tombs and the connected belief system which is possibly the oldest belief system, forgotten in time, may have been an initiatory, Gnostic belief system.

Gnosis means 'knowledge' and this is the underlying factor lying at the hub of all the Gnostic religions. Knowledge that is by personal spiritual experience, not of academic learning, but the personal experience which comes from an encounter with the Divine.

This personal experience would have often been received through the mystery schools, who would pass down the ancient knowledge through teachings and interaction with symbols, with the aim of speaking directly to the subconscious mind or the collective subconscious.

In the late 1950s the eminent psychiatric and analytical psychologist Carl Gustav Jung, wrote of this 'reservoir of the experiences of our species';

"My thesis, then, is as follows: In addition to our immediate consciousness, which is of a thoroughly personal nature and which we believe to be the only empirical psyche (even if we tack on the personal unconscious as an appendix), there exists a second psychic system of a collective, universal, and impersonal nature which is identical in all individuals. This collective unconscious does not develop individually but is inherited. It consists of pre-existent forms, the archetypes, which can only become conscious secondarily and which give definite form to certain psychic contents'. (Excerpted from The Archetypes And The Collective Unconscious by C. G. Jung.)

When they were ready the candidates would be passed through a ceremony, which would always be characterised by a ritual death and rebirth. In some cases the candidate would be isolated in a ritualised tomb to allow the whole process time to sink in whilst the candidate was alone both personally and spiritually. They would then be removed from the tomb and ritually re-born or born-again, often after three days and would then be considered 'initiated' into whatever level of the teachings they had been studying.

This process is analogous with the sun's progress through the time of the solstices, or 'stand-stills'. After travelling through the sky during the year and setting further northward or southward each day, it eventually reaches its solstice positions on June 21st/22nd in summer and December 21st/22nd in winter. In the Gnostic tradition, the sun is said to 'die' at this point as it remains still in the sky for three days, when it is said to be 'born again', as it restarts its journey back through the skies; a story with obvious similarities to the Christian story.

All the mystery schools, with the exception of Mithraism (which was mainly followed by the male soldiers of the Roman army), would be available to anyone who wished to make the journey, whatever status in the community and whatever sex.

Although early Christianity was a Gnostic belief system, this changed at the Council of Nicaea. In Britain the early Christian teachings, which became known as Celtic Christianity, lasted much longer and were only absorbed into the orthodox church much later at the synod of Whitby in

664AD under the influence of St Wilfred the associate and bogus mentor of Dagerbert II.

The chart below shows the main differences between Gnostic Christianity and the new orthodox or conventional Christianity introduced after the council of Nicaea under the Nicene Creed.

Conventional Christianity	Gnostic Christianity
Faith "The substance of *things* hoped for, the evidence for *things unseen*"	**Gnosis (Knowledge)**
Creeds (believed to be literally true)	Myths (allegorical stories)
Uniformity in belief	Diversity in belief
Organisation of the church	Experience of the individual
Control of thinking	Individuality of thinking

Dualism

The other defining characteristic of Catharism is dualism; the standard, orthodox interpretation of which, involves a belief in two Gods; the creator God of the Old Testament, who the Cathars viewed as evil and the benevolent God of the New Testament. It is a common belief though, that the Cathars were the holders of a great body of esoteric knowledge, passed down through the ages and that it was this collected wisdom that the Catholic Church went to such great efforts to silence and keep from taking hold.

It is clear through, from the teaching of the modern day mystery schools, that the concept of dualism extends much further than merely the notion of good verses evil and that duality is in effect the basis of a much wider philosophy. The basis of which is an appreciation that we are living in an experience of opposites on every possible level of our understanding. For example we experience; up/down, in/out, black/white, dead/alive, small/big, day/night good/evil and so on. In fact everything in the universe has its opposite and this is the defining aspect of our experience in this reality we see around us. This is an extremely difficult concept to express, but a look at well known symbols, such as the Cabbalistic Tree of Life, would maybe provide some insight into the idea of duality.

Yin & Yang and the Black & White squares

Also the Yin and Yang sign represents the meeting of the opposites with the spots relating to the idea that each opposite contains a little of its counterpart. The chequer board, which is recognisable from many ritual locations such as Free Masonic Lodges, represents the same thing. The Kabbalistc 'Tree of Life' contains three pillars; the pillar of severity is the left hand or female pillar; the pillar of mercy is the right hand or male pillar and the central pillar is the pillar of equilibrium. It is on this central pillar, which represents the coming together of duality that a candidate for initiation would aim to raise to higher spiritual plains.

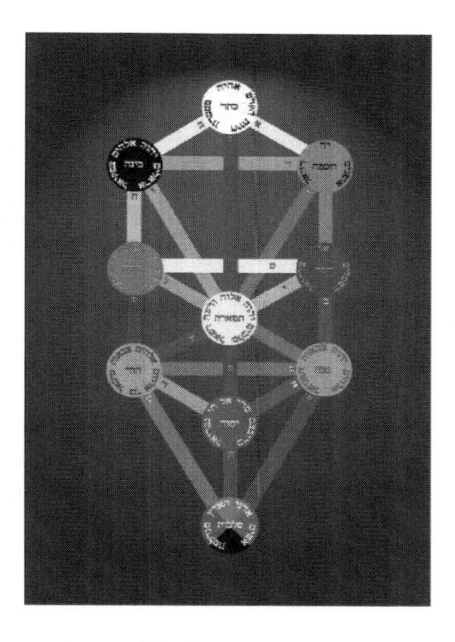

The Cabbalistc 'Tree of Life'

The fate of the Cathars
The Albigensian Crusade

The Occitan residents of the early 12th centaury Languedoc would be more than used to seeing wandering troubadours and traders arriving in their towns and villages and amongst them certain pairs of travellers, recognisable by their black robes tied round the waist with a leather thong. They would arrive in town and set up shop, often as weavers or other manual trades and would earn reputations as hard working holy-men, honest in their business dealings and would eventually gain an audience amongst the surrounding citizens.

They would begin speaking to small groups around the town and on invitation in local homes. They asked for nothing as they believed in hard work and self sufficiency. The word would soon spread, in these land of tolerance and absence of persecution and eventually the following of these Bon Christians, became measurable in their thousands.

The Cathar teachings probably originated from the much earlier Bogomils, a dualist creed from Eastern Europe around the area of today's Bulgaria. The Cathar leaders sometimes referred to as 'the monks-in-the-world', were properly known as Perfects, or perfected ones, or the fully initiated. These were the old souls on their last reincarnation into this world, which it is said they believed to have been created as evil. It was this teaching, which was the most important bugbear to the Roman church as it led to the belief that Jesus did not exist in the flesh, but was in fact pure completed spirit. This was in total contrast to the Orthodox Church's creeds and was therefore considered by them to be heretical.

The Cathar Country

Cathar Perfects teaching the locals.
From the Hurepel museum, Minerve

In contrast the Cathars thought that the real teachings of Christ had been sabotaged at the council of Nicaea and that this had led to them being buried away and lost to mankind. They also believed that on this earthly plain, our sprits were imprisoned within the earthly body and that we had to make a good end in order to break the cycle of reincarnation and return to limitless light, a process which we would all eventually complete. To this end the Cathar Perfects would give the 'Consolamentum' to believers, either as a last right or to initiate them as new Perfects.

The Cathars rejected the Orthodox Church with all its sacraments and regarded all the images and finery of church buildings and priests as totally pointless. They regarded the cross as the instrument of Christ's torture and found the church's habit of cross veneration to be repulsive. They also rejected the belligerent deity of the Old Testament as being associated with the evil creator of the earth.

An ordinary believer was encouraged to live according to the teachings of Christ but apart from that they were free to live their lives as they wished. Like most monks, the Perfect's abstained from sex, prayed constantly, and fasted frequently. They were vegetarians and avoided any result of reproduction; ie milk, cheese, butter and eggs, but could drink wine and eat fish. Any deviation from this regime would mean that they were no longer perfect and would have to retake the Consolomentum, when ready. But most of all the Cathars were peaceful, tolerant, hard working and attempted to live good basic lives.

All this would be enough to ruffle the feathers of the church, but it is also thought the Cathars held a great and holy secret, which had the potential to rock the very foundations of the Roman church.

What this secret was we still don't know, but it was thought that it included a sacred manuscript called the 'Book of Love'. This manuscript was said to hold many secrets of alchemy and the ancient mysteries, which taught of how to transmute basic man into spiritual being. According to Catharic belief, one object of earthly life was to make over the human body as a worthy vehicle for the light of the Holy Spirit. The point was to know the Grail not as a cup but as a process, to which Jesus was the model.

The Cathar Country

Whether it was the covering up of this secret, which led to the reaction of the Roman Church, or whether it was enough that this, so called heretical sect was threatening its power base in the area? The reaction came in 1145, with a visit to the Languedoc by the most important and influential churchman of the day, Bernard of Clairvaux, a leader of the Cistercian order and friend to the powerful families of the area.

Bernard went on a preaching tour of the Languedoc, but this was cut short in the market place of Verfeil, when his preaching was drowned out by sound of mounted knights clashing their swords together. He was laughed out of town and returned to Champaign.

Then around the turn of the 13th centaury, after the Count of Toulouse had refused to intercede with the Cathars amongst his people, on behalf of the Roman church, the decision was made to debate the Cathars on their home territory.

Catholic priests travelled to the Languedoc and held discussions in the great halls of the lords and castle courtyards. Local lords guaranteed safe passage for both sides of these massive debates, which included such subjects as the role of the church, the devil, the meaning of humanity's existence, the meaning of time and all perceivable theological subject matter. If things had not changed, these amazing debates, taking place in these lands characterised by free thinking and religious tolerance, would have gone down as one of the greatest ever events in the history of religious philosophy.

The Priests and the Perfects argued for days and weeks at a time and crowds grew in their thousands, but the Orthodox

Church was gaining little ground. It was clear to the Occitan populace that the outright corruption of the Roman church in the Languedoc and the policy of levying heavy taxes on the local population, which sustained the lavish life style of the priesthood, was in stark contrast to the simple lives of the Cathars. Then unfortunately, due to the churches lack of converts and the inability to convince the populace to convert in any numbers, the Catholic Church ran out of patience.

It is from this point that the infamous words of Domanic Guzeman the founder of the Dominican Order, stretches back to us through history;

'Preaching and entreaty have failed us, now you will receive the stick';

and what a stick this was to be. The holy Roman Church set about instigating the first European genocide, which would involve the cold blooded murder of thousands of good Christian people, for the crime of not agreeing with the church and wishing to live good, honest and peaceful lives.

On March 10th 1208, Pope Innocent III called for a crusade against the Cathars. The crusade was to be preached by Arnold Amaury, who set about rallying support from the French, who occupied the lands to the north of the independent Languedoc.

At first the northerners had no interest in invading the southern lands having no quarrel with them. Innocent eventually won them over with promises of forgiveness of all sins past and future, which gives a free hand to do anything you like. He also promised all the captured lands of the

The Cathar Country

Languedoc to the northern lords and that all past debts would be written off.

The armies of the Pope marched on the lands of Raymond Roger Trencavel, the 24 year old viscount of Albi, Carcassonne, Bezier and all the surrounding lands. His family was ancient, powerful and known to be just. His uncle, Raymond VI, Count of Toulouse, after many unpleasant encounters with the Pope's men over recent years, which had led to him being publicly flogged, in front of the church at St. Giles, had swapped sides. Whether he had done this to protect his people or not, this was a severe blow to Raymond Roger Trencavel.

Beziers

The City of Beziers and the Bridge over the River Orb

The Cathar Country

As the armies of the north congregated on the plains below Beziers, the young lord rode to Montpellier to parley with Amaury and to attempt to reach some sort of compromise, but to no avail. The Bishop of Beziers was part of the crusade and it was he, who was to arrive with the final ultimatum. It contained a demand to produce 222 Cathar Perfects to the crusade for punishment, which of course meant to be burned alive. The reply was swift, 'we would rather drown in the salty sea than to change anything in our government'.

On the morning of 22nd July 1209 the Biterrois, those who stood on the walls of this great city of Beziers, sitting on the banks of the river Orb, looked out over a sea of crusader armies. They stretched out as far as the eye could see; a terrifying and awe inspiring sight. The crusaders were settling in for a long siege against this mighty and seemingly impregnable city.

Then fate played its hand! A few young camp workers wandered over the Orb Bridge and found a place to relax in the sun near to the city walls. They shouted insults up to the watchers on the walls above and this proved too much for some of the city youths. They foolishly opened a gate in the wall and ran down the slope towards the river to teach the jeering intruder a lesson. They beat him and threw him into the Orb, making just enough noise to sound the alarm. The gathered hoards heard the shouting and saw the open gate. They set off in their hundreds towards it as the young Biterrois fled back up the embankment. The crusaders were on them before they could make the gate; they had made an unbelievable mistake. The siege was over before it was even begun.

The Cathar Country

As the call to arms went round the camp, the message soon reached the church men in charge. It was at this point that the infamous words were spoken by Arnold Amaury 'Caedite eos. Novit enim Dominus qui sunt eius' 'Kill them all. God will know his own'. The crusaders did as they had been commanded by the highest representative of the Vicar of Christ. They turned the city into an abattoir and butchered the entire 20,000 inhabitants. This amount of slaughter, in the days before gunpowder, guns and rifles would have taken a huge amount of effort.

Arnold Amaury wrote to Pope Innocent of their success, 'nearly twenty thousand of the citizens were put to the sword, regardless of age and sex. The workings of divine vengeance have been wonderful'.

Stephen O'Shea makes the ominous point that;

'A threshold had been crossed in the ordering of men's minds'. ('O'Shea, Stephen, *The Perfect Herecy'*, P.87).

The Cathars had received their first stick!

Carcassonne

Raymond Roger Trencavel had arranged for the plains between Beziers and Carcassonne to become barren, so that the crusader armies would not be able to live off his people's lands. All the crops were burned, windmills demolished and all the livestock slaughtered.

The armies arrived at Carcassonne on the morning of August 1st, after taking time off to celebrate the feast day of St. Mary Magdalene. Their first act was to attack the outlying city to the north, catching it and cutting off the water supply to the city.

A surprise appearance of King Pedro II of Aragon from across the Pyrenees, called a halt to proceedings. Pedro was Raymond's liege lord and part of his feudal family. He was known as a good catholic and under normal circumstances the king's council would have been considered important. This was his jurisdiction and he should have had the final say in the fate of his vassals.

Carcassonne and the group of June 2009

After pleading with Raymond to sort out the situation with the Cathars, Pedro called an audience with the leaders of the

The Cathar Country

crusade, confident that the historical laws of feudal society and custom would prevail and that some sort of compromise could be reached. Most of the northern lords would have been on the side of Pedro and would have been looking towards the end of their 40 days of service and heading home.

But it was Arnold Amaury, who was in charge of the Pope's crusade and his answer was a further insult. His terms were that Raymond Roger could leave the city with eleven others of his choice and with whatever they could carry. The fate of the city and its inhabitants would then be left to the crusaders. Pedro, appalled with this intended insult, replied that 'donkeys will fly!' When hearing Amaury's reply, Raymond retorted that 'it would be better to be flayed alive than to acquiesce in such a base betrayal of his people'.

The following day the siege engines came into play, the city was secure and the siege was set for a long haul. As the intense heat of the summer in the South of France roared on, it was taking its toll. As the weeks rolled by, the siege fever started taking hold, exacerbated by the scarcity of water.

Then without any warning a lone horsemen approached the walls of Le Cité, he shouted up at the guards on the wall that he was a kinsman of the Trencavels and that he wanted a parley with the lord of the City. The name of this lone visitor was not recorded in history, but the author can't help but put the name of Raymond Count of Toulouse into the frame.

The crowd gathered around when Raymond Roger heard the message which began sympathetically, 'I hope that you and your people will prosper. I will certainly advise you to hold out if you are expecting relief to arrive soon. But you must be aware that nothing of that kind will happen'. This was followed by a thinly veiled threat and then an offer of safe conduct to the pavilions of the French to negotiate.

Raymond Roger took his kinsman at his word and rode out of the city alone. It is thought that he was met by the northern lords, in the way that honour and chivalry had historically dictated. Unfortunately Arnold Armaury was in charge and had other ideas and Raymond Roger Trencavel was to loose his freedom.

The people of Carcossonne were told to leave the city through a narrow gateway carrying nothing but the shirts on their backs. It may be asked why the process was drawn out in this way, when a main gate would have been considerably more efficient. Were the Pope's people looking for anyone or anything in particular? The people of the city dispersed over the plains, towards the hills along the river in the intense heat and into history.

The city was to be re-inhabited and the new lordship of Carcassonne was offered to many and was refused by many, as this great prize was not won in honour, but treachery. On the 15th August Simon de Montford became the new Viscount of Bezier, Carcassonne and all of the Trencavel lands between.

Simon de Montfort

De Montfort moved into the Chateau within the walls of Carcassonne accompanied by forty knights and an army of several hundred. From this base he set about the job of subduing the lands of his knew fiefdom, which was of course, inhabited by thousands of his enemies.

His first act of public administration was to instigate a crippling poll-tax, with most of the proceeds being sent to the Pope. If de Montfort had any ideas of winning round the hearts and minds of the populace, then this was not going to help. After all how were the people supposed to earn the money needed to pay the increased demands of the churches coffers from vineyards and crops, which were being regularly burned by de Montfort's armies, let alone make any sort of a living?

The Towers of Chateau Lastours

The town of Cabaret become a refuge for many of the displaced of Carcossonne, who had made their way to this place, which was already becoming a strong hold of resistance. The town was also going to be the first place on de Monforts list, as his early attempts to subdue it were completely thwarted and he was sent packing. The wild lands surrounding Lastours, or 'the towers', was not suitable for siege encampment as the towers were standing above two steep valleys.

De Montfort then went about loosing 40 of the original 100 castles which had been captured by the crusade. This was beginning to be an embarrassment for the new lord and it seems that he decided that a message needed to be sent to his unruly minions.

The event occurred in the town of Bram, which was constructed on a circulade or castrum town plan; a circular terraced design with off-set streets leading to a central public area. The aim of this design was to fend off marauders and bandits in the way that a wagon train would form a circle to defend against attacking natives in the Wild West. This was no defence from the armies of de Montfort, who took the town after just three days of light siege work.

The town of Cabaret was nearly 25 miles from Bram and news of the loss of the town was delivered in a fashion so macabre as to defy words, leaving only a factual description possible. At the defeat of Bram de Montfort had taken 100 prisoners and had set about on a grisly process of disfiguration. He had their ears and their noses cut off with their top lips. He then had all their eyes gouged out except for one prisoner who was allowed to keep one eye. He was to be the group leader. They arrived at Cabaret as a gruesome procession, exhausted and stumbling, all in a line with one arm out and with their hand on the shoulder of the one in front. The hideous sight must have been a terrifying and ghoulish spectacle of grimacing, walking skulls.

The town of Minerve

De Montford continued his onslaught on the lands of the Cathars, moving from town to town and village to village. At the ancient town of Minerve, where 1,200 years earlier, the philosopher Pliny the Elder (AD 23-79), greatly admired the wines from the vineyards of the Minervois, which grow on the slopes surrounding the Citadel, the bombardment was merciless. De Montfort had engaged the use of a huge new siege engine called 'La Malvoisine', the Bad Neighbour! The sheer size of this brute and the damage it was causing by emptying its immense payloads onto the citadel was enough to encourage a raiding party to cross the divide in the dead of

The Cathar Country

night with the aim of setting fire to the engine. The daring attempt unfortunately failed and William of Minerve was forced to negotiate terms with de Montfort. William offered all his lands over and in return Simon de Montfort, in an unusual act on lenience offered a minor valley fiefdom to William and a free exit for his people.

The two warriors were about to seal the deal, when Arnold Amaury arrived on the scene and immediately intervened. Arnolds clause in the agreement was that the inhabitants of Minerve, could leave the town but only after they had denied Catharism, adding 'Don't worry; you will see that very few of them will convert'. On 22nd July 1210, exactly a year since Amaury had ordered the massacre at Bezier, 140 Cathars were lead down the mountainside and onto a pyre and tied to stakes, whilst the kindling beneath their feet was set alight. The mighty Church of Rome had thought of another method of carrying out Christ's will, with the mass murder of 140 Cathars by burning them alive. It is interesting that it was again on the feast day of St. Mary Magdalene that Arnold Amaury chose to up the stakes!

Simon de Montfort's crusade then focused his attention on the Chateau at Termes. By August 1210 the castle had been surrounded by a whole mass of siege engines, which had been dragged over the barren road-less landscape. A small band of resistance fighters from Cabaret attempted a raid, with the aim of burning the engines, but they were seen off by the crusaders and did not manage to regroup sufficiently to have any real effect. In September Raymond of Termes, lord of the area, began to negotiate a surrender, but an early winter downfall refilled his water supply and uplifted the defenders spirits. They managed to hold out until November 23rd, when the castle was finally abandoned secretly in the middle of the night. In an unbelievable move Raymond of Termes then turned around and slipped back into the castle and when de Montfort moved in to claim his quarry, he was arrested and ended his days in the dungeon at Carcassonne.

After this the crusade moved through the lands of the Languedoc taking the smaller towns and castrums such as Albedun, which was eventually to have a second life as the Knight Templar preceptory of Bezu. By the new year of 1211 most of the Tencavel lands had been taken by de Montfort and even the hill top centre of resistance at Cabaret had finally given in, for a promise of leniency from the new lord of the lands at Carcassonne.

Toulouse

After a winter of rest, de Montfort had evidently decided that the Trencavel lands would not suffice and he turned his attention to the lands of Raymond Count of Toulouse. Throughout the campaign so far Raymond had been playing the delicate game of appearing to be part of the crusade, whilst inwardly hoping that this would be enough to keep the invaders from his lands. He even led a delegation to Rome for an audience with the Pope, pleading leniency and the chance to sort out his lands to the satisfaction of the church, in order that he be left alone to run the lands of Toulouse in peace.

In January 1211 King Pedro of Aragon brought his mighty hand into play, in an attempt at peace in the Languedoc. In an unprecedented act he made Simon de Montfort his vassal, thus recognising his claim to the ancestral lands of the Trencavels.

He laid down one condition, that Raymond VI Count of Toulouse would be reinstated firmly in his rightful position of lord of his own ancestral lands and to be allowed to rule uninterrupted.

Arnold Amaury gave his reply at a council in Montpellier on 4th February 1211. He kept the king and Raymond waiting outside the church until eventually the holy reply had to be brought out and read by one of the waiting entourage.

The contents of the reply included; the count must forsake the use of mercenaries, pay taxes to the clergy, levy no tolls, stop employing Jews and deliver all heretics to the crusaders within one year. Also all of the castles and fortresses in his lands were to be demolished. Raymond and his subjects were forbidden to eat meat more than twice a week and they all had to wear coarse brown robes and the nobles would have to move out of their homes into the country to live as peasants working the land. All of their property, goods and possessions would be offered to the crusaders and Raymond him self would be exiled to Palestine. The church had in fact stated that the lands of Toulouse must follow the lands of the Trencavels into their possession.

It was April 1211 when de Montfort took to the road again. This time he headed to the town of Lavaur on the boarder between the lands of the Trencavels and the Toulouses, a land where Cathar Perfects peacefully lived and worked. The siege which surrounded the town was having little effect due to a shortage of manpower. Reinforments of 5,000 troops, which were expected to man the siege, had been ambushed by the men of Raymond-Roger of Foix. After a month de Monfort's men managed to move a siege engine called a Chatte (or cat),

The Cathar Country

which formed a wooden shelter, over to the perimeter of the city and began to undermine the walls, or dig beneath the foundations.

On breaking into the city one of their first acts was to throw Dame Guiraude, the Lady of Lavaur into the well, whilst still alive. They then threw stones on top of her until she stopped screaming. They then attempted to hang her brother Aimery of Montreal, but when the scaffold collapsed, de Montfort ordered his throat be cut, together with all eighty of his knights. The next act of the crusading forces was to burn alive up to 400 Cathars on a mass pyre, all in the name of Christ. The city was then ransacked and all the possessions became the property of the Catholic Church.

De Montfort proceeded in this general manner increasing the size of his lands, with little to stop him. King Pedro of Aragon attempted another diplomatic intervention with Innocent III, at the beginning of 1213 and on 17th January he managed to convince the Pope to call off the crusade in the Languedoc leaving the king in overall control and ordered de Montfort to hand back some of his lands. Unfortunately the hand of Arnold Amaury then came into play again and after much complaining that the Cathar heretics were still very much at large in the Languedoc, the crusade was reinstated on 21st May.

De Montfort also reinstated his campaign of what had turned into a total land grab and empire building. On 12th September a huge battle ensued at Muret, not far from Toulouse and King Pedro himself was killed along with 7,000 of his men. De Montfort was now the unopposed lord of the whole of the Languedoc. This was effectively confirmed at the Fourth

The Cathar Country

Lateran Council in Rome, when in mid December 1215, it was declared that Simon de Montfort could keep all his lands in the Languedoc and was now the official Count of Toulouse. This was the last intervention of Innocent III, who died on 16th July 1216.

Whilst the Pope had granted the city of Toulouse to de Montfort, the people had different ideas about who was going to lead them. Simon de Montfort was roundly hated and the city of Toulouse had become the home of the deposed of the Languedoc and the refuge of those who had suffered at the injustices of the crusade. On his return to Toulouse the new count besieged the city. He was willing to destroy Toulouse, murder everyone in it and then build a new one near by. Who he intended to live in his new city, history does not tell.

The Count Raymond of Toulouse, whilst being pretty much muted by the holy verdict at the Lateran, had one weapon left in his arsenal, his son. Raymond VII was a natural general and in the summer of 1216 he set about leading an opposition to the church. On taking back the city of Beaucaire, on the banks of the Rhone and on the border between the Languedoc and Provence he was known to have stated that 'the Church had no business depriving him of his birthright'. Simon sped over to Beaucaire to teach the 'boy' a lesson and found a man, who repeatedly sent him packing.

Whilst de Montfort laid siege to Beaucaire his problems got worse with the news of the death of Innocent III in Perugia. To top this, resistance at Toulouse was getting the upper hand. He raised the siege at Beaucaire and raced back to Toulouse to regain control of the city. It appeared that the gift of Pope Innocent had become a curse as the new count was severely over stretched. He had just made himself too many enemies and would rather butcher than talk. The taxes levied on his people were crippling and were in place to pay for a defiant war over his own lands, which may not have been necessary if he had not been such a tyrant.

Having apparently subdued Toulouse de Montfort made the mistake of many criminals. He got greedy. He had taken the ancestral lands of the lords of Trencavel and now Toulouse, but he was not satisfied and started looking over the border to Provence. He set off in November leaving Toulouse under martial law and in his absence the people regrouped and began building up a silent militia. Then on 13th September 1217 Raymond VI left his hideout in the Pyrenees and set off for Toulouse. He rode the whole way from the mountains without detection with a small group of his men and gained entrance to the city to much celebration; 'now we have the morning star risen and shining upon us! This is our lord who was lost'. Raymond ordered the people to rebuild the defences of the city, which they set about doing with renewed hope.

A chronicler wrote of the city's activity;

'Never in any town have I seen such magnificent labour, for the counts were hard at work there, with all the knights, the citizens and their wives and valiant merchants, men, women and courteous money-changers, small children, boys, girls, servants, running messengers, every one had a pick, a shovel or a garden fork, every one of them joined eagerly in the work. And at night they all kept watch together, lights and candlesticks were placed along the streets, drums and tabors sounded and bugles played. In heartfelt joy, women and girls sang and danced to merry tunes'.

The Cathar Country

The dreaded Simon de Montfort returned on 8th October and without hesitation instigated a full on attack on the city. As usual the Pope had his senior representatives amongst the host to make sure that Christ's work was done during the crusade. In fact the leading bishop was recorded to have said 'let neither man nor woman escape alive'.

Unfortunately for the work of the holy church, the citizens of Toulouse had prepared for this very moment and were determined not to Succomb to either the holy sword nor to holy imprisonment under a French tyrannical leader. De Montfort's army firstly fell against the prepared defences and then as they struggled, they had to face a full frontal cavalry attack from Roger Bernard of Foix and his men. De Montfort's men were soundly beaten back and for the next six months did not stop trying to take the city, with the same result.

Simon attempted to siege the city, but his shortage of men and the very size of the city worked against him. Also the city sits on the river Garonne, which provides a plentiful supply of water. The crusaders tried attacking the city from every conceivable direction, from east, west, over the bridges and through the river, but they just could not break through the defences. In what must have been a state of growing frustration and anxiety, de Montfort called to the French lords for a final crusade against the Cathars and they came. But even with these vastly increased numbers de Montfort still failed to gain access to his own capital city.

Then as if to add insult to injury Raymond VII, the younger, managed to pass through the whole crusader army unseen and entered the city to much applause and celebration.

The Cathar Country

By the middle of summer it was getting to the time when the northern reinforcements were ending their 40 days tour of duty and would be heading home. If de Montfort was going to take Toulouse then he was going to have to do it soon and he knew it. His strategy was to have a huge chatte constructed; one the likes of which had never been seen in the Languedoc. The city's defenders could see the danger presented by this big cat and decided to take early preventative action. They dropped their ladders over the walls and scrambled across the moat and up the bank, making headway towards the chatte. De Montfort's men rushed up to meet the raiding party, joined by Simon himself, but only after he had finished mass. The defenders quickly retreated back to the wall having smashed the chatte, leaving the crusaders in the firing line for the catapults and archers on the walls.

At this point fate intervened and de Montfort's brother was felled. As de Montfort rushed over to him and dismounted, he was hit full on the head by the payload from a mangonel operated by women of the city. This time the city really celebrated, it was Monday 25th June 1218 and 'Lo lop es mort' – 'The wolf is dead!'

In the Canso de la Crosada (Song of the Cathar wars), it is written:-

'There was in the town a mangonel built by our carpenters
And dragged with its platform from St Sernin.
It was operated by noblewomen,
by little girls and men's wives,
And now a stone hit just where it was needed
Striking Count Simon on his steel helmet

Shattering his eyes, brains, and back teeth,
And splintering his forehead and jaw.
Bleeding and black, the Count dropped dead on the ground'.

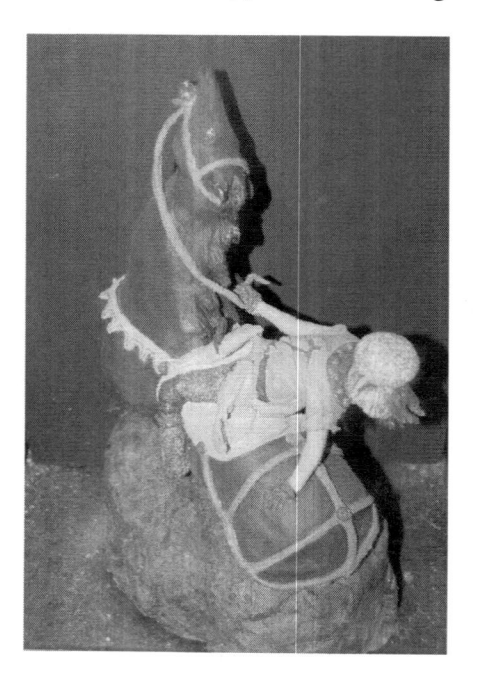

Simon de Montfort is felled
From the Hurepel museum, Minerve

Simon de Montfort, the scourge of the Languedoc was interned at a service at the Cathedral of St. Nazaire in Carcassonne. Some of the residents of the Languedoc can quote the final words of the Canso de la Crosada, even today:-

'The epitaph says, for those who can read it,
That he is a saint and martyr who shall breathe again

*And shall in wondrous joy inherit and flourish
And wear a crown and sit on a heavenly throne.
And I have heard it said that this must be so –
If by killing men and spilling blood,
By wasting souls, and preaching murder,
By following evil counsels, and raising fires,
By ruining noblemen and besmirching paratge,
By pillaging the country, and by exalting Pride,
By stoking up wickedness and stifling good,
By massacring women and their infants,
A man can win Jesus in this world,
then Simon surely wears a crown, respondent in heaven'.*

After the death of de Montfort the siege was lifted within a month, which was characterized by little activity and from this time the people of the Languedoc actually had the upper hand.

Cathar Perfects began coming down from the mountain top citadel of Montsegur, which had become a retreat for the heretics during the crusade. The sight of dark robes would again be seen in the streets and weaving shelters would reappear in the open areas of the towns and cities. Peace and freedom was breaking out again in the Languedoc.

Inquisition

In 1227 a new pope was elected in Rome. Gregory IX was concerned about the spread of heresy but had a new way of dealing with the problem. In 1233 he was to set up a process of heresy courts and he was to put the whole thing in the hands of the Dominican Order. These courts became known as the inquisition.

The Cathar Country

Depiction of a Cathar Perfect before the Inquisition
From the Hurepel museum, Minerve

As the inquisition started to get organised a significant early case occurred in Toulouse. An old lady lay on her death bed and asked to make a 'good end', which meant that she would like to take the consolamentum, or the Cathar last rights. Her servants quietly made their way to the local Cathar house and brought a Cathar Perfect who performed the consolamentum and left as cautiously as he had arrived.

As all this was happening another member of the household sneaked out to the Dominican monastery and reported the situation to one William Pelhisson, the inquisitor. The informer told the tale of a dying woman in a state of delirium calling for the Cathar Perfect. William, together with Raymond du Fauga and the other friars were having their mid day meal, but could not resist this heresy only a few doors from where they were feasting. They all made their way to the house of the woman where they crept upstairs to her room. A family member whispered that the Lord Bishop had arrived, but it seemed that the lady of the house misunderstood and addressed the bishop as the Cathar Perfect. The Catholic bishop did not correct her but instead began to question her as if he was in-fact the Perfect and allowed her to incriminate herself as a member of the Cathar faith.

The bishop then declared the lady guilty of heresy and condemned her to execution. They then lashed the lady to her bed, carried it out to the street and in a procession beyond the city gate, where they set fire to it with the lady still tied in. Having burned alive a women who only had hours to live, the bishop and his friars returned to finish their dinner.

The inquisition moved through the Languedoc like a plague, accusing and burning hundreds in its wake. The Cathar Perfects tended to move to safe places away from the constant threat of the Dominicans and the spectacular mountain top citadel of Montsegur became a popular and important retreat and centre for Cathar work.

Montsegur

By the early 1240s Montesgur was the home of nearly 500 people; including 200 Cathar Perfects led by Bertrand Marty, seeking a peaceful place of safety. Other occupants included members of the family of Raymond of Pereille, who was lord of Monsegur. Their was also a doctor by the name of Arnaud Rouquier and his family, who were soon to be under great demand and the citadel guard, which consisted of twelve knights, fifty-five sergeants, a catapult expert, the commander Pierre-Roger of Merpoix and their families.

The mountain-top citadel of Montsegur

The Cathars would come and go travelling the lands in pairs, one senior perfect and one pupil. They are recorded to have worked as weavers, bakers, cobbles and millers.

It was late spring when the men of the Pope and the French king started arriving at the base of the mighty Mountain of St. Bartholomew which held Montsegur high on its summit. The siege was instigated and organised by Hugues des Arcis, the seneschal of Carcassonne.

As the summer months drew on the devastated defenders heard news that the Count of Foix had changed sides and joined the crusade. They had one hope left and that was that reinforcements would arrive in the shape of Raymond of Toulouse, who was known to be in Rome trying to negotiate with the Pope. To this end messengers were sent down the mountain and through enemy lines. Within a couple of weeks a fire was lit on a nearby mountain signalling that Raymond would be back in the Languedoc within the year.

Summer turned to winter and whilst the siege was holding Hugues des Arcis was having doubts. Soon the valleys and slopes would be covered by a blanket of snow and this would make his job extremely difficult. He decided that he had to make some headway if he was going to have any chance of success. To this end he gathered together a small group to climb the treacherous Roc de la Tour, a sheer face of rock beneath a small plateau. Incredibly they reached their goal in the middle of the night with the help of local guides and mercenaries from the Basque region. The plateau sentries could never have expected such a daring raid and were caught off guard; the invaders killed them before setting up camp. It is said that the following morning the raiders looked back down their ascent path and swore in fear that they would never have attempted such a thing if they had seen it first.

Montsegur was now in the range of siege weaponry and the attackers wasted no time; they began winching engines up to the plateau and the bombardment of the citadel began. As the constant pounding continued to demoralise the inhabitants, it must have seemed inevitable that defeat was only a matter of time away. It was getting near to Christmas and Raymond Roger of Toulouse and his reinforcements were nowhere to be seen. The Cathar Church had amassed a huge wealth at Montsegur over the years, including not only gold and silver

The Cathar Country

but also religious treasures, whatever they might have been and Bernard Marty decided that this treasure should be removed to safety. It was decided that a pair of Cathars, one Perfect and one Deacon should slip down the mountain, taking the treasure through the attacking army's camps and to safety.

The daring evacuation took place a few days before Christmas and was successful apart from an encounter with a group of sentries, who luckily for the Cathar escape party, were local mercenaries and Cathar sympathisers and they let them pass. The treasure was successfully delivered to a safe 'spoulga' or fortified cave, in the county of Foix.

Back in the besieged citadel of Montsegur, morale was ebbing and many believers entered into a pact with the Perfects so that they would make a 'good end'. It was agreed that they would perform the consolamentum on any of the believers who had become too injured to speak the required ritual replies.

The attackers had been steadily gaining ground and by Christmas they had advanced to within around 60 yards of the citadel, after taking a treacherous circular path along the edge of the mountain to the base of the barbican, the outer fortification just outside the main walls. The job was not finished though as the castle had been designed with protection in mind and in order to reach the inner defences the attackers would have to cross a 6 foot wide corridor exposed on both sides to sever drops. As the catapult attacks continued the result seemed inevitable, the small group of around one hundred fighting men defended against a siege army of up to 10,000.

The Cathar Country

In the new year of 1244 a couple of dozen reinforcements arrived at Montsegur from nearby Usson and Pierre-Roger of Merpoix told Raymond of Pereille that he thought they could hold out until Easter, a date which it seemed was important to them. Unfortunately things did not improve and by the end of February no reinforcements had arrived and it now appeared that they never would. Then on March 1st 1244 a single horn was heard from the citadel walls of Montsegur, after ten months of bombardment the siege was over. Raymond and Pierre-Roger walked down the mountain of St. Bartholomew and surrendered to Hugues de Arcis and Peter Amiel, the archbishop of Narbonne.

Negotiations were swift as both sides were weary after a long winter and the terms of the treaty were agreed within a day. The results were unusually lenient in some respects, in that all but the Cathar Perfects had any past crimes forgiven and they could all go free, after they had been interrogated by the inquisition. The Perfects however had to renounce their faith or be burned alive. The final clause in the treaty was by far the most unusual; a two week truce was requested by the defenders before any further action was to be taken. This was granted as part of the agreement, but the question which has reverberated through time is why after been bombarded during a ten month siege, after an excruciating winter, after the evacuation of their treasure and after having plenty of time to make peace with their God did they want a further two weeks?

As the years have rolled by many theories have been offered to this enigma. It has been suggested that the timing of Easter may have played a part in the decision, but as the Cathars did not venerate the cross nor believe in Christ as flesh, this would appear extremely unlikely. Then there was the potential significance of the date of the spring equinox. In many pagan belief systems it is usual to observe certain rituals around this time, which presently falls around the 21st March in the Gregorian calendar. But in 1244 the Julian calendar was still in use and the equinox fell on 14th March just before the end of the two week truce. It was on this day that twenty-six mercenaries, knights, soldiers and followers of the Cathar faith actually asked for the consolamentum thus condemning themselves to the pyres of the Roman Church. This act, maybe more than any other during the persecution of the Cathars indicates the level of commitment and belief of the members of this Church, which was Christian even though not in a way which was deemed acceptable by the Church of Rome.

It is widely believed that the Cathars had in their possession certain holy relics, artefacts and manuscripts including early mystical teachings, which lay at the heart of their beliefs and which had been passed down through countless generations. Possibly even the holy grail its self was included amongst the Cathar relics and if the grail is the alchemical secret of how to convert base humanity into the pure gold of spiritual enlightenment, then perhaps the Cathars did posses this secret.

Whatever it was that the Cathars held so dear and whether or not it was involved in a spring equinox ritual, it is certain that it was smuggled out of Montsegur. Records tell of how four Perfects either made their way through the enemy lines or were lowered with ropes down a sheer cliff and escaped the citadel carrying the Cathar secrets to safety. They made their way to a nearby 'spoulga', or fortified cave, where they met up

The Cathar Country

with Mathieu, the Perfect who had secreted the treasure out of Montsegur and they eventually hid all the valuable possessions of the Cathars in the castle at Usson some 30 miles away, until this stronghold its self was eventually abandoned.

Then back at Montsegur at dawn on the 16th March 1244 the two week truce was coming to an end. Around 220 Cathars, some having only received the Consolomentum two days earlier, walked in procession down the track to a clearing at the base of the mountain. Here Hugues des Arcis, Governor of Carcassonne and Peter Amiel, Archbishop of Narbonne waited with murderous intent.

The Cathars, who had been shackled together for their 300 metre decent to death, would have been watching the progress of the construction of the instrument of their execution over the two weeks of the truce. The huge wooden palisades were now in place and as the Cathars approached the pyres, firewood fagots soaked in pitch were being piled amongst upright stakes. The sorry procession of Bon Christians, led by the elderly Bertrand Marty, made their way bare foot and dressed in coarse garments towards their death. Their prayers were drowned out by the chanted psalms of the Catholic monks, priests and bishops. The Perfects were tied to the stakes like wild boar on a spit. As the fires took hold, the spitting and hissing sound of burning fat and the screams of pain from the dying Christians were drowned out as the singing of the Catholic faithful got louder.

This was a wonderful day for the Roman Church and the Catholic Chronicler Guillaume recorded: 'Refusing the conversion to which they were exhorted, they were burnt in an enclosure made of sticks and stakes which was set on fire and despatched them to the fire of Tartarus'. The work of the god of Rome had again been carried out to great effect.

Today visitors to Montsegur and Beziers are struck by the atmosphere of these places where such tragedy is woven into the very fabric of the land and buildings.

Monument to the Cathars at the foot of Montsegur

The last days of the Cathars

The burnings at Montsegur heralded an end to the fight for religious freedom in the Languedoc and although the people would cherish secret dualistic beliefs, fear had won the day. One milestone in the control of humankind had been reached. From this point on, the inquisition went from strength to strength as terrified Occitans denounced friends and family members as the bush fire of fear spread in the hearts of these once free people.

Yet through the darkness of tyranny one voice remained to shine the lantern of the hermit, which the Cathars believed had shone for the fathers of mankind, for Jesus of the Nazarene sect, for Mary Magdalene and for the people of the Languedoc, through the long years of the crusade and then through the inquisition.

William Belibaste did not fit the usual Cathar mould and in earlier days he would have had to retake the consolomentum on a regular basis to maintain his role as a Perfect. But this was over 100 years since the fall of Beziers and the Cathars were now counted on one hand instead of in their tens of thousands.

Belibaste came from a landed Cathar family of peasant farmers and grew up with his bothers on the hill slopes of the Corbières. But William was as rugged as the slopes where he fought for a living as a shepherd and he was known to have murdered a local man who was going to denounce one of his brothers, who was already on the to-do list of the inquisitors. Whilst hiding in the hills the two brothers soon met up with other fugitives of the summary judgement of the Pope's men.

Amongst this band of Cathar brothers was the Perfect, Philip d'Alayrac and it was he who taught Belibaste the Cathar mysteries and eventually performed the consolomentum, bringing him into the ranks of the Perfects. After being captured by the king's men and thrown into the cells in Carcassonne in 1309, they amazingly managed to escape and fled over the mountain border into Aragon, where they settled in a small community of Occitan refugees. When his mentor Philip d'Alayrac was captured and burned alive, William the shepherd boy from the Corbières, had his first flock of Cathar souls.

Belibaste took on the appearance of a married man by cohabiting with Raymonda Piquier, a ruse which, whilst designed to ward off inquisitive eyes, also became a reality and the two eventually had a child together. Never the less Belibaste was a good leader and religious teacher, although he refused to administer the consolomentum, as he recognised his flawed status as a Perfect.

In his uplifting sermons he spoke of avoiding the sin of despair and of the love of God and the need to replicate this between each other. He worked hard to lead and support his followers and was known as a good and honest man.

Eventually the community found a place to settle in Morella and Sant Mateu on the river Ebro, around 200 miles from their original homes. At last the wandering Cathars had found a place they could call their own.

Then in 1317 the community took on a new member by the name of Arnold Sicre, who joined them as a shoe maker and apparently became an avid follower of Belibaste. Sicre appeared to be contented with his new life but spoke often of his Cathar aunt and sister left behind in the Languedoc Mountains near Andorra. Belibaste sent Sicre on a mission to bring them to the community, but he returned alone after many months of absence with news and a request. His aunt was too ill to travel but would like the blessing of a Perfect before her death and she would also like to make a substantial

The Cathar Country

donation to the exiled community. As for his sister, she had been provided with a large dowry and was anxious to meet a certain young Cathar suitor, who had been found for her amongst Sicre's new friends. On his return to the community Sicre reported that his relatives had requested a visit from Belibaste and his closest associates.

Against advice from his friends and comrades Belibaste planned the journey back to the Languedoc. It was the spring of 1321, when he gathered together a small party of fellow travellers including, Arnold Sicre, Arnold Marty (the prospective husband) and the shepherd Peter Maury.

Although Belibaste appeared to be taking Sicre on good faith, he must still have harboured doubts because he attempted to ply him wine at a river side inn, in order to check his story whilst he was intoxicated. Unfortunately Sicre saw through the 'in vino veritas' plan and continually emptied his drink elsewhere than down himself. The foiled plot was hatched by Maury suggesting to the apparently drunken Sicre that they betray Belibaste and collect the reward. Sirce of course feigned outrage, putting the party at ease and confirming their trust in him.

The truth of Sicre's treachery would soon become apparent and it ran deeper than Belibaste could have imagined. Sicre had been an interloper from day one and in the employ of the Bishop of Fournier, the Inquisitor of Pamiers, who was destined to become Pope Benedict XII. Sicre's arrival at the community in Catalonia and his fictitious aunt and sister was all a plan of the bishop. He was to become accepted, collect evidence and eventually deliver the leaders to the inquisition.

The Cathar Country

All had worked according to plan and in a morning raid in the village of Tirvia, where the party had spent the night; they were rounded up and arrested. Sicre would be handsomely rewarded with cash and the return of his family property which had been confiscated by the church. He was to become an extremely rich man.

Belibaste was convicted of heresy and in the Corbières village of Villerouge-Termenes, in the autumn of 1321, he walked head held high into the village courtyard, climbed a pile of straw and vine cuttings and was tied to a stake. As the flames took hold, they engulfed the body of William Belibaste releasing the soul of the last remaining Cathar Perfect from its earthly bondage.

It was a hot July morning of 1209 in Beziers, when the Pope's representative had uttered the infamous words 'kill them all'. It had taken 112 years of tyranny, torture and murder in the most sickening and horrifying ways for the god of the Catholic Church to complete its task. The heart of mankind had learned a whole new lesson in fear, but it had taken over a century for the church to break the souls of a courageous people.

In modern times it is hard for the hierarchy of the Church to justify the exploits of the Inquisition, so its name was changed to 'Congregation for the doctrine of the faith'. From 1981 to 2005 the position of Prefect of this order, the title of which used to be the Grand Inquisitor, was one Joseph Cardinal Ratzinger, who was to become Pope Benedict XVI in 2005. This was 671 years after Jacques Fournier, the Inquisitor of Pamiers was elected Pope Benedict XII in 1334 after the burning of William Belibaste.

The Cathar Country

Excommunications from the Catholic Church under Ratzinger's conservative prefecture continued at an alarming rate, as he strove to suppress the views of clerics and theologians who questioned Catholic dogma on such modernising issues as birth control, abortion, divorce and Papal infallibility.

Chapter 4

François Bérenger Saunière and the Mystery of Rennes-le-Château

Coustaussa Castle with Rennes-le-Chateau in the background

The most famous mystery of the Cathar Country is a story which has been told to children in the Languedoc and Aude Valley for generations and a story which is today told worldwide. The scene for this intriguing tale is the tiny hill top village of Rennes-le-Château. This serene little hamlet used to be the mighty Visigothic city of Rhedae, which would stretch away over the hillside and into the valley bellow. Today the village appears innocent enough at first sight, but this place has a history and this place holds secrets, many secrets.

The Cathar Country

The sign post from the D118 through Couiza is pretty unexceptional. It reads Rennes-le-Château 4.5 kilometers and following its direction you begin to climb and you climb and you climb, passing views of Coustaussa Castle, Mount Cardou, the Knight Templar mountain top Château de Bezu and the Templar Château de Blanchefort in the near distance. Finally you reach the summit and encounter the first of the village's ancient buildings, the impressive Château which used to be the home to the Hautpoul-de-Blanchefort family, a family with strong Templar connections. Bertrand de Blanchefort was the sixth grand master, holding the office from 1156 to 1169.

The Cathar Country

Château de Blanchefort at Rennes-le-Château

Having made your way through a couple of narrow streets you find your way to the car park and are stunned by the spectacular panoramic views. Next to the car park is the enigmatic Tour Magdela and the mystery begins because this was the domain of the infamous priest François Bérenger Saunière.

François Bérenger Saunière

François Bérenger Saunière
(1852-1917)

Saunière was a local lad from just across the valley from Rennes-le-Château. He was born in the small town of Montazels on 1st April 1852, into a reasonably well off family. His father was not only the estate manager for the Marquis de Casemajou, but also the director of the local flour mill, as well as once holding the position of Mayor of Montazels. The comfortable family income resulting from the varied occupations of his father was enough to provide an education for Bérenger and his six younger siblings. His brother Alfred followed him into the priesthood and his two younger brothers both had a university education, taking up careers in medicine and the law.

The Sauniere House in Montazels (centre)

Much writing about the Saunière mystery describes a pennyiless priest, but it can be clearly seen that Bèrenger came from a relatively middle class background and in fact when he entered the priesthood he had gathered healthy private savings of 600 francs, quite a sum in the late 19th century.

Bérenger Saunière loved the outdoors. He spent his childhood and teen age years exploring every last inch of his beloved Aude Valley. He would hunt with his father and fish for fresh water shrimp in hidden ponds and tickle trout in the many fast flowing springs. He would have known the rich history of the area and is known to have spent time hunting for the lost treasure of the Visigoths. He would have heard the story the 'poor shepherd boy' Ignace Paris, who in 1645 appeared in the village of Rennes-le-Château with his pockets full of gold. The villagers cross examined the young lad, but when he refused to reveal the source of his newly acquired wealth they stoned him to death.

It would appear that Bérenger had an ideal and happy childhood with a firm family background and a beautiful countryside play-ground. The man who entered the priesthood seems to have been strong willed, determined, healthy, robust and extremely self-assured. He was ordained in 1879 at the age of 27 and received his first posting to the quiet and historic, small town of Alet-les-Bains. Then after a short time as curate of Le Clat, he finally arrived as priest of Rennes-le-Chateau on 1st June 1885, at the age of 33.

Sauniere's Astrological Profile

The following astrological summary was provided by Duncan Harpur, the president of the Manchester based astrological society 'Phoenix Rising'. It provides an extremely interesting personality profile of Saunière and helps in understanding his motives. Of particular interest is the insight into the 'dichotomy' present in his personality. This could explain to some extent how he could be a member of an extremely conservative organization (the church), whilst at the same time appearing to go his own way, both personally and religiously

The Profile

It could be said that each of us wears a mask when facing the world and through this mask we filter our sense, feeling and thought impressions into our core being. In Saunière's case the world often appeared rather threatening and like the crab, he was careful when coming out of his shell to gauge the temperature; if it felt too cold or warm then he recoiled. A lot of the time he wore this shell to the world to mask his emotional vulnerability.

He could be sympathetic with a genuine empathy and his presence had a soothing quality on an environment. When called on to act confrontationally or when feeling threatened he would take a one step forward and two steps back approach, always looking for another way of approaching an issue, as he realised there was a flaw in every situation or person. He would try to find the least adversarial means to achieve his goals. He clung on to financial and emotional security, even when it wasn't always in his own interests. He was intensely secretive and kept areas of his life distinct, introducing individuals to each other only if he felt it really necessary.

He had a lot of raw energy that needed to be channelled in both direction and application, as his will needed to be stabilized. His timing in being in the right place at the right time was spot on, due to intuitively recognising potential opportunities and being able to see the bigger picture. He preferred to lead others, but not from a power or control perspective, but to do what he wanted without others making demands. His desire to be himself on his own terms meant he needed less social reinforcement than most.

He was not one for emotional displays unless it was enthusiasm, assertiveness or anger. His anger was rather like a steam kettle; every so often he needed to burn off energy, but he soon calmed down. The matter would be then concluded and he wouldn't remember the reason for the explosion minutes later. He would have been impatient and lacked persistence and stamina if obstacles stood in his way. One of his qualities was an unwillingness to act deceitfully or dishonestly due to a desire not to be misrepresented.

He was a "personality" rather larger than life and enjoyed leading rather than following. He preferred being on the go then sitting around waiting for something to happen; inevitably with this outlook on life events did happen. He knew what he wanted and the shortest route to attaining it and he could be extremely competitive, wanting to be first. He was proud of his courage, daring and ability to accomplish. His impetuosity and impulsiveness, jumping into matters head first led him into making some big mistakes. He used his fighting ability in assisting others who were less able than himself; otherwise he would have been too confrontational. Sorting things out peaceably wasn't what he was about, but he certainly got things moving.

Saunière had a weakness in his thinking function. He wouldn't have been particularly rational in his decision making. Once he had decided on a course of action he wasn't disposed to changing his mind or seeing matters from a different perspective. He was very much an action orientated person who made sure he got things done. He had a strong need to be correct from society's standpoint which would have caused turmoil given the Bishop of Carcassonne wanting him to appear before him on a regular basis to explain the origins of his finance. He did however take his case to the Pope for acceptance by the church; so although a maverick in some ways, he didn't like authority and would undermine it if he could; there was a strong conservative streak running through him. This dichotomy must have been difficult to live with.

He was a man that in the end was noticed, but he needed the approval of others; he could be rather arrogant and a bit of a know it all. He needed emotional security and his housekeeper would have been rather more than her job description stated. He took on responsibility easily, but he could be a bit of a workaholic and dark moods would sometimes descend. He could be ruthless where necessary and rather cruel especially if he had been abused, where he could wreak revenge on innocent bystanders. He enjoyed physically demolishing things. He would end up feeling ostracized from polite society.

Background to the Mystery

On taking up the living at Rennes-le-Château, Saunière arrived in the village to find the church of St. Mary Magdalene in near ruin and the Presbytery uninhabitable. But Saunière had a determined character and he decided that his first job was to be one of renovation. So after taking lodgings with the Dénarnaud family, he quickly used up his personal savings of 600fr mending the church roof, which leaked rain water onto his altar. After this the church accounts recorded him

The Cathar Country

borrowing money from the Dénarnaud's in order to carry on the church renovation project.

The days of the late 19th centaury were uncertain times both for the royalty and the church. Revolution fever lingered in the air after the monarchy had nearly been reinstated only a short time earlier. The republican movement had tasted blood and now had the added objective of removing the power of the Catholic Church and anti-clerical feeling was rife in the populace.

It was in this atmosphere that Saunière delivered this powerfully pro-royalty sermon on the eve of the country's general election, in October 1885;

'My dear brethren, the Republic is asking us to elect our Representatives. We mustn't lose such a wonderful chance to get rid of this evil institution with the very weapons it's given us. Any method is good – even legitimate – to crush this wicked regime! The Republic is the Devil's work. The blood of our Kings stains the Republicans' hands. And now they want to bring down the Catholic Church and – make no mistake – if we don't get rid of them, they'll do everything they can to make it happen. I'm talking especially to you, my dear sisters, so that, when you get home, you can explain to your husbands the danger facing our church; the danger facing our children, deprived of a religious education… and the danger to our very souls, exposed as they are to such godless and revolutionary propaganda. If the Republican Party defeats the Royalists, I can see dark days ahead for our church and for our Country.'

Dark days were indeed ahead for the church and in 1905 the Republicans achieved separation of church and state. For Saunière the consequences of his outspokenness were a little more immediate. Complaints from the Republicans in the village, led by the school master resulted in his stipend being suspended and on the 1st December 1885 he was transferred to teaching duties at the Junior Seminary in Narbonne.

Whilst in, what must have felt like exile on the Mediterranean, Saunière visited his brother Alfred frequently. Alfred had somewhat followed in his fathers footsteps and after being ordained into the priesthood, had gone into the service of the Marquis de Chefdebien, working as tutor to the counts children.

It is at this point that fate played its hand in a way that rocked Saunière's world and has sent reverberations down through history, which can still be felt today. The chain of events had begun a generation ago with the connection between the Saunière family and the Chefdebien dynasty, which started when Bérenger's father had gone into the service of the Count.

The Marquis of Chefdebien had been a great personal friend of the late Comte de Chambord, the heir to the throne of France, who had turned down the opportunity to reign as King Henry V, after the previous elections. It was said that the Count did not wish to be the source of ongoing division in France and the bloodshed, which would have undoubtedly resulted from the restoration of the monarchy.

Even more importantly the widowed Countess de Chambord was still alive and she was a member of the Hapsbourg family, which at the time was the most powerful family in the world, economically, politically and religiously. It was with this powerful connection that Saunière was promptly reinstated to the position of priest of the village of Rennes-le-Chateau.

The Cathar Country

When he arrived back in the village in 1886 he had with him a personal gift of 3,000fr from the Countess of Chambord, heir to the throne of France, herself. He also arrived back with a mission, maybe a royal mission!

The question has to be asked; what interest could Marie-Therèse of Austria, the Countess of Chamborg, the one-time pretender to the throne of France and one of the most influential people on the planet, really have in a meagre village priest? What was the motive for this gift, which would have been equivalent to five years salary to Saunière. Was this just a gesture of good-will to a royalist supporter, or did the great lady and her family want something in return?

The answer to this riddle would appear to lie in the history of Rennes-le-Château and in particular the Hautpoul-Blanchfort family who used to be a hugely powerful Cathar family in the Languedoc. The Blanchfort family home was the château at Rennes and the church of Mary Magdalene was their family chapel. It is widely believed that the Blanchfort's had a family secret, which had been passed down through the generations, but the origin of this secret has never been openly revealed.

It is possible that the early activities of the Knights Templar may shed some light here. For the first nine years of their existence after the order was formed around the first decade of the 12th century, the Templars expended a huge amount of energy digging beneath the Temple Mount in Jerusalem and it is widely believed that they found what they were looking for. What the content of this discovery was, whether it consisted of manuscripts, relics or both, the Templars would have removed their find to safer places.

The Cathar Country

Bertrand de Blanchefort of Rennes, had been a member of the Templar Order for some years before he became a highly influential Grand Master in either 1153 or 1156. At the beginning of his 17 years in office, de Blanchefort organised for a contingent of German speaking miners to be brought to area around Rennes-le-Château. The foreigners worked under the strictest of security on the slopes of Mount Cardou, 'the holy mountain' as well as the slopes beneath the Templar observation point of Blanchefort opposite. Because the miners were involved in smelting operations on the mountains it is highly probable that they were concealing something rather than removing anything. In any case any mines, which were once profitable on the slopes, had been exhausted years before by the Romans.

Whatever the nature of the secret, it was in danger of being lost for Marie d'Able, marchioness of Hautpoul de Blanchefort was the last of the family to hold the secret. Marie had fallen out with her children and so had to find a totally reliable confidant, who would understand the full ramifications of what she had to pass on. The person she chose was the Abbé Bigou, the priest of Rennes-le-Château for the previous 20 years. In 1781 Marie de Blanchfort died, leaving Bigou holding the family secret, but within 10 years the priest was having unexpected problems of his own and his position had become uncertain.

It is somewhat ironic that the difficulties facing Bigou, were the same as the problems facing Saunière, the priest who took his place at Rennes-le-Château a hundred years later. This was the time known as the Terror, Republicanism was strong and the guillotines (the Widows) were working overtime. The rivers of the Seine were running red with the blood of the Lords and anti-clericalism was rife.

Antoine Bigou decided that his only option was to flee France and in the late summer of 1792 he set off on foot to the Village of St. Paul de Fenouillet at the end of the spectacular Gorge de Galimus, where he crossed the border into Spain, never to return. Luckily Bigou was as a man of honour and he understood the importance of the documents, which had been entrusted to him by Marie de Blanchefort. He had spent the two months before he left, hiding away all the secrets around the church. He did, of course have a dilemma. He wanted the secret to remain hidden, but knew that it needed to be passed on to the right person at some time in the future. As we shall see Antoine Bigou was a highly intelligent and ingenious man.

But the connection between Bigou and the Blanchforts is not the only one of significance to our story. It was 52 years after Mary de Blanchfort passed her family secrets onto Antoine Bigou and 52 years before they were discovered by the other priest of Rennes-le-Château, Bérenger Saunière, that the young Duke of Bordeaux, the future Compte de Chambord, pretender to the throne of France, was introduced to a member of the Hautpoul-Blanchfort family. Constant Amand d' Hautpoul, whose great-aunt was Mary de Blanchfort became tutor to the thirteen year old Duke. This encounter began a relationship, which developed into a firm friendship over many years.

Amand d' Hautpoul told the Duke of the Blanchfort family secret and how it had been passed on and hidden at Rennes-le-Château. The Duke eventually told his wife the Countess de Chambord and it was she, who before her death in 1886,

The Cathar Country

passed the message onto Bérenger Saunière, through her friend the Marquis de Chefdebien. It is also highly probable that the Countess would have passed the information onto her uncle the Hapsburg Emperor of Austria, whose family motto is 'Austriae est imperare orbi universo', or A.E.I.O.U. (it falls to Austria to rule over the whole globe). To anyone concerned with the study of the so called, New World Order and the centralisation of money and power, this declared goal by one of the worlds leading families, must appear as quite a revealing statement.

As would be suggested from the Languedoc's extensive history of religious diversity and tolerance recorded above, the area was fertile ground for the plethora of secret societies which had sprung up all over France around the end of the 18th centaury. Some of these organisations may have been politically benign and focused mainly on the spiritual development of their initiates, but others were most certainly not! These societies would bring together some of the most influential aristocratic families of the region with highly politicised goals.

At this point it is sufficient to note the way in which the names associated with the various groups indicate connections between the families involved, which could be important in understanding and interpreting the Saunière story.

In 1780, which was around the time that Mary de Blanchfort was passing her family secrets onto the Abbé Bigou and the year before she died, the Marquis Francois Chefdebien was forming the secret society known as 'The Philadelphians' in Narbonne, which was involved in the study of occult science. Then in 1838 Jacques-Etienne, the Marconis de Negre, a relative of the de Blanchforts, began a society called the 'Rite of Memphis' in his home town of Montauban. Jacques-Etienne had been an initiate of the 'Rite of Misraim' in Vienna for around five years, a country which was awash with alchemy and the study of occult philosophy at the time.

Three other members of the Blanchfort family; Charles, Eugene and Theobold d'Hautpoul, were initiates of the 'Legitimist Masonic Lodge of la Sagasse', in Toulouse around 1840. Toulouse was known as the occult capital of the Languedoc at the time and the numerous lodges in the city held a variety of opinions and goals, but it was the royalist 'Wisdom' lodge to which the Hautpouls held their allegiance. It was the aim of the 'Wisdom Lodge' to support the royalist cause and in particular the Bourbons, whose family head would have been the very same Henry V, Comte de Chamborg, who we have earlier connected with the Sauniere family, through the Marquis of Chefdebien.

The stream of occult learning and philosophy continued in the Languedoc up to Saunière's day and beyond. 1845 saw the formation of the 'Order of the Rose Cross of the Temple and the Grail' and in 1888 three Occitan gentlemen occultists, including one Doctor Gerard Eucausse, or 'Papus' instigated the 'Kabalistic Order of the Rose Cross'. Then in 1891, the year that Saunière made his great discovery, another of the three occultists began the 'Order of the Temple and the Catholic Order of the Rose Cross'. The heavily Rosicrucian influence to the secret societies of the Languedoc can easily be discerned from their names, but this latter society would appear to indicate that a Rosicrucian and therefore, Masonic influence existed within the catholic church of the area.

The mystery unfolds

The Pillars

François Bérenger Saunière returned to Rennes-le-Château in the middle of 1886 after around seven months of enforced exile in Narbonne. His stipend had been reinstated and he had the 3,000 gold francs gifted by the Countess de Chambord in his pocket. He was a man with a reinvigorated mission and as soon as the parish was back in order after his absence, it was time to recommence work on the church.

Employing the services of the quality glass makers, 'Feur of Bordeaux', Saunière had all the stained glass windows replaced in style, before turning his attention to replacing the giant recumbent stone slab, which had been used as an altar since the Visigothic period. It has been widely speculated that it was during this process that coded parchments were found in a carved groove in the Visigothic pillar which supported the altar, although it is also possible that the parchments were found later during the replacement of the pulpit.

Saunière eventually had the Visagothic Pillar moved to the church yard where it was turned upside down and the carved words 'Mission 1891' were added above the original carved Visigothic 'cross of secrecy', which adorns the main face of the pillar. In some occult circles the reversing of a symbol may indicate that it is worth looking beyond the immediate to find a different, deeper or hidden meaning. Saunière and his predecessor Bigou seemed to understand this principle extremely well.

The Cathar Country

The Visigothic Altar support and Wooden Pulpit Support

Today the original pillar can be found and examined in the Rennes-le-Château museum and the one in the churchyard, holding up a statue of 'Our Lady at Lourdes' is a copy. Examination of the original pillar reveals that there is in fact a small recess on the top which may have held a fixing tongue on the alter slab. Alternatively the cavity could have been a 'caspa', a hollow groove carved by the stone masons of Catholic Churches, to hold relics and ceremonial documents from the church's consecration, together with a few lucky coins. It would appear extremely unlikely that this particular hollow would have held anything of any great importance to our mystery.

The kitty of 3,000fr soon began to diminish and although the work on the church continued it took on a slower pace. Then in 1891, a full five years after Saunière's return to Rennes, it was the turn of the old 17th century pulpit to retire and make way for a new flying St. Sulpice type construction. It was during this process that the church bell-ringer, Antoine Captier recovered the carved wooden support pillar, which used to hold up the old pulpit. As Antoine moved the pillar from the rubble pile, a glass phial fell from a secret notch, which had been cleverly carved in the decorative head. The phial smashed on the floor, revealing a roll of old parchments which he duly delivered to the Abbe Saunière.

Bérenger had the impressive carved pillar moved to the library he had commissioned within the Tour Magdala, where it remained for the rest of his life. Maybe it served as a reminder of the moment he was handed the parchments, because it is clear that things were never going to be the same again for the priest. In fact from that moment on things changed dramatically.

Today the pillar is on display in the Rennes-le-Château museum, on loan from the Captier family. It is made of hard chestnut and the groove had remained intact since the days of the Abbé Bigou, when it was probably carved by either Bigou himself or on his behalf, in order to hide the parchments before he fled to Spain. A wedge of softer wood had been carved to fit into the slot to keep the whole thing hidden. In the 100 years it had been in position, the softer wood had probably rotted away causing the parchments to reveal themselves as the pillar was removed. If Bigou had planned the parchments to reveal themselves in this way he was ingenious indeed.

The Parchments

Which ever pillar the parchments were found in, the mystery says that in the summer of 1891 Saunière had in his possession four old documents. Two of the documents are said to have been genealogical lists and two were sections of the New Testament, probably written out by the Abbé Bigou a hundred years previously and altered to include a hidden coded message.

It appears that after much burning of the midnight oil; Saunière was unable to translate the parchments so he took them to his immediate superior and friend, the Bishop Billard of Carcassonne. Although the task proved too great even for this distinguished scholar, Billard must have recognised something of importance in the parchments. Saunière was immediately dispatched to Paris to seek the assistance of the experts in the translation of cryptic texts at the Seminary of San Sulpice.

It appears that our provincial priest was to fit in very well with the metropolitan city set during his three week furlough. The Seminary Director General Abbey Bieil introduced him to his nephew, Emile Hoffet who, whilst training as a priest, was heavily involved in the various occult organisations and secret societies, which abounded in the capital at the time. Saunière appears to have been warmly welcomed into this inner circle and in particular by the famous opera singer Emma Calvé with whom he is said to have been extremely close. Calvé purchased and restored the Château de Cabrières in 1894, a property with a rich and deep occult history which had previously belonged to her family. It was at Cabrières that the occult text 'Abraham the Jew', that had formerly been owned by Nicholas Flaumel, was safely secreted away for many years. The property was eventually sold to a former private tutor to the Hapsburgs in Calvé's latter years.

Evidence that Saunière's mission in Paris to translate the texts was successful was provided by Gerard de Sede in 1967, when he reproduced copies of the parchments in 'The Accursed Treasure of Rennes-le-Château'. The documents were claimed, by de Sede, to be tracings of the originals kept by the mayor of Rennes-le-Château after he had received them from Saunière himself.

The first parchment which has become known as the 'Dagobert' parchment is the shorter of the two and consists of a compilation of Gospel texts about Jesus and his disciples eating corn on the Sabbath. The translation of this parchment was relatively simple as it involved the translation of several letters that had been separated from the main text. It was Henry Lincoln who first recorded this as;

'A DAGOBERT II ROI ET A SION EST CE TRESOR ET IL EST LA MORT'

'To Dagobert II, King, and to Sion is this treasure and he is there dead'. (Baigent, Leigh and Lincoln, *The Holy Blood and the Holy Grail.*)

The Cathar Country

```
ET FACTUM EST EUM IN
SAbbATO SECUNdo PRIMO A
bIREPERSCCETESdISCIPULIAUTEM ILLIRIS COE
PERUNTUELLERE SPICASET FRICANTES MANIbUS + MANdU
CAbANT QUIdAM AUTEM dE FARISAEIS dT
CEbANTE!ECCE QUIA FACIUNT dISCIPULI TUI SAb
bATIS + QUOd NON LICET RESPONdENS AUTEM INS
SETX IT A dE OS NUM QUAM boC
LECISTI SQUOd FECIT dAUId QUANdO
ESURUT IPSE ET QUI CUM EO ERAI + INTROIbITIN dOMUM
dEI ET PANES PROPOSITIONIS        REdIS
MANdUCAUIT ET dedIT ET QUI          bIES
CUM ERANT UXUS QUIbUS NO
NLICEbAT MANdUCARE SI NON    SOLIS SACER dOTIbUS
```

The 'Dagobert' parchment

The second parchment known as the 'Shepherdess' parchment involved a far more complicated and drawn out chain of decipherments which finally results in;

'Bergère pas de tentation. Que Poussin Teniers gardent la clef. Pax DCLXXXI (681). Par la croix et ce cheval de dieu. J'achève ce daemon de gardien à midi. Pommes bleues'.

'Shepherdess no temptation. That Poussin (&) Teniers hold the key. Peace 681. By the cross and this horse of God, I complete this guardian daemon at midday. Blue apples'. (Baigent, Leigh and Lincoln, *The Holy Blood and the Holy Grail*.)

The Cathar Country

The 'Shepherdess' parchment

Before Saunière returned to the Languedoc he visited the Louvre and purchased reproductions of three paintings, two of which appear to have a definite connection with the translation of the Shepherdess parchment. The first painting was a portrait of Pope Celestine V. by an unknown artist. But Saunière also probably purchased a copy of David Teniers 'St. Anthony and St. Paul in the Desert' as the translation states 'no temptation' and this is the only one of Teniers painting depicting St. Anthony NOT being tempted.

The Cathar Country

The final painting was Nicolas Poussin's 'Shepherds of Arcadia' which appears to refer to the Shepherdess in the translation and which also seems to portray the landscape around the Aude valley and a tomb that used to be found near the village of Arques. An inscription on the tomb in the painting reads 'Et in Arcadia Ego', which translate as 'Even I in Death am in Arcadia'. Tim Wallace-Murphy suggested that the phrase should be further transcribed as an anagram to reveal;

'Et In Arca Dei Ago' or *'And I act on behalf of the Ark of God'*. (Tim Wallace-Murphy, *Rex Deus*).

Nicolas Poussin's 'Shepherds of Arcadia'

The Cathar Country

Is the Ark of the Covenant, which was stolen from Solomon's Temple by the Romans and then recovered from Rome by the Visigoths, hidden somewhere in the landscape shown in the Shepherds of Arcadia painting? In this theory of the Shepherds of Arcadia the white mountain to the right of the trees is said to represent Mount Cardou. The next peak being Blanchfort were the Visigoths, then the Knight Templar had a chateau overseeing the holy mountain. As discussed above, Mount Cardou has an early and profound connection with the Ark.

Nicolas Poussin resided in Rome for his entire life but in 1640, the year ascribed to the painting of the Shepherds of Arcadia, he took a trip to Paris. History does not reveal whether Poussin took a detour to the Languedoc en-route, but evidence does exist that he had a secret of some sort. In a letter dated 17th April 1656, from the Abbé Louis Fouquet in Rome to his brother Nicolas Fouquet, the Superintendent of Finances to Louis 14th in Paris, the Abbé wrote:

'M.Poussin... and I discussed certain things which I shall with ease be able to explain to you in detail. Things which will give you, through M. Poussin, advantages which even kings would have great pains to draw from him and which, according to him, it is possible that nobody else will ever rediscover in the centuries to come; and what is more, the matter involves little expenditure and could even be turned to profit, and these are things so difficult to discover that nothing now on this earth can prove better value nor its equal...'
(Lincoln, Henry, The Holy Place)

Some time after receiving this letter, Nicolas Fouquet became extremely rich, much in the way Saunière did over 200 years later. It was thought that his wealth and life-style equalled the king he served. Not surprisingly, considering Fouquet's employment in the royal treasury, his new found income led to suspicion. In 1661 he was arrested and sent to Pignerol in the Alps of Savoy, where he was held in the dungeon of the fortress until he died under unusual circumstances on 23rd March 1680, some 19 years later. This unusually harsh treatment of a previously trusted and honoured member of the royal household was at the express intervention of the king, who overruled the original courts decision to acquit Fouquet. This was the only time in French history that the head of state used powers provided to pardon an offender, to increase the sentence instead of reduce it. It is probable that the desired effect was to ensure that any secret that Fouquet had uncovered went with him to his grave.

After his death his two prison guards found themselves unexpectedly imprisoned. Their warders were given instructions that the prisoners were to be kept in total isolation in one room. They were to have no communication with anyone, either in speech or writing. The king is also said to have purchased a copy of the Shepherds of Arcadia having spent much time going through Fouque's personal papers. This painting was never put on public display, but was kept in his private quarters.

Discovered a Tomb – Rain in the Afternoon

On returning to Rennes-le-Château, Saunière got straight back to work on the church of St Mary Magdalene, but now with the added knowledge he had gained at the seminary of San Sulpice.

With the assistance of two local builders, Adrien Marre and Felicien Marceau, Saunière immediately pointed out a flagstone which he had the builders lift up from the floor of the church in front of the altar. The stone was larger than the others around it, measuring around four feet by two feet and turning it over revealed wonderful Carolingian carvings from the seventh or eight century.

The Carolingian Knights Stone (La Dalle des Chevaliers)

On the evening of September 21st 1891 Saunière made an enigmatic entry in his diary, 'Letter from Granes. Discovery of a tomb. Rain in the evening.' This appears to refer to the discovery of a tomb beneath the Knights Stone, as it has become known, that contains the remains of the ancient Seigniors of Rennes-le-Château. The presence of the tomb was confirmed by an entry in a parish registry, written by the Abbé Bigou;

'The tomb of the Seigniors is to be found to the right of the baluster'. (Robin, Jean-Luc, *Rennes-le-Chateau Sauniere's Secret*).

All other village archives were destroyed in a fire, but in an ironic twist, that particular journal, which also records the death of the Marquise de Blanchefort, appears to have been removed and probably hidden by Saunière and is therefore the only one left to be read today.

A further document written by Jean Bigou, the uncle of Antoine Bigou, who preceded him as priest of Rennes-le-Château, must have been an inspiration to Saunière in his searches and is still revealing to us today.

'Beneath the altar of the church of Rennes-le-Château there is a chamber in which are tombs dating from the times of the ancient kings, as well as documents which must not fall into unintended hands, I have had the access to this crypt sealed'. (Robin, Jean-Luc, *Rennes-le-Chateau Sauniere's Secret*).

Could these hidden documents contain part of the secret that the Countess of Chamborg had commissioned Saunière to recover, for the Habsbourgs, from the church and did he find them inside the tomb beneath the Knights Stone?

What we do know is that the tomb contained the proverbial pot of gold and that Saunière was not in the mood for sharing. On discovering the gold he immediately dismissed his builders, telling them that the pot merely contained useless religious medals from Lourdes. After discovering the tomb Saunière's activities increased in intensity. He barricaded himself inside the church where he carried on his explorations unobserved. His investigations eventually expanded into the graveyard where he and Marie Denarnaud could be observed digging at all hours of the day and night.

The primary focus of Saunière's cemetery related activities was the grave of the Mary de Blanchfort which was indicated by two large stones, both carved by the Abbé Bigou. The stones were removed to the edge of the cemetery where Saunière expended a great deal of effort in chiselling away the inscriptions and destroying the hidden messages they contained. As fate would have it though, the cemetery had been visited around 1880 by an M. E Cros, who had taken a rubbing of the gravestone and recorded the inscription in the 'Revue of the Archaeological Society of the Aude' and so we still have a record of it today.

An entry in Saunière's journal on 29th September 1891 reads 'Saw the cure of Nevian. Visited Gelis and Carrière. Saw Cros and Secret'. This shows that he caught up with M. Earnest Cros and in-fact he became firm friends with this long-established freemason. What the secret was and who he shared it with is not mentioned, but the Abbé Gelis became part of the inner circle and was murdered in extremely strange circumstances six years later.

The Cathar Country

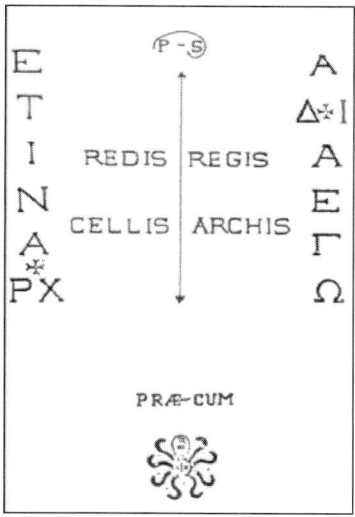

The Headstone(above) and a copy of the Gravestone of Mary de Blanchfort

Interpretation of the Headstone

When the Abbé Bigou had this stone inscribed he saw to it that, whilst at first glance it appeared as a badly carved stone, on further examination the many minor errors produce interesting results.

Firstly it is quite astounding that the inscription on the headstone is an exact anagram of the final translation of the Shepherdess parchment with 'PS Praecum' added. This has to be confirmation that the translation is correct...

> 'Bergère pas de tentation. Que Poussin Teniers gardent la clef. Pax DCLXXXI (681). Par la croix et ce cheval de dieu. J'achève ce daemon de gardien à midi. Pommes bleues - PS Praecum'

The second result is possibly the more important as it provided a missing key to the decipherment of the Shepherdess parchment. Eight letters on the headstone have been carved out of position, four capitals 'MORT' and four lower-case 'epee' and it is this word, which can be translated as 'Death-Sword', which is the required key. In 'Mysteries of Templar Treasure & the Holy Grail – The Secrets of Rennes-Le-Chateau', Lionel and Patricia Fanthorpe say that they have discovered that with a couple of minor changes the translation could also be 'emprunte', meaning false or borrowed. This could have many interpretations including an indication that the inscription should not be taken at first sight but that it requires a deeper reading.

Interpretation of the Gravestone

An interpretation of the gravestone is best carried out in three stages. Firstly the four central words are Latin and are probably best translated as 'At royal Reddis, in the store-rooms of the fortress'. Reddis being the old Visigothic name for Rennes-le-Château. So what is to be found in the store-rooms of the fortress?

Here we can consider the second element of the puzzle, the PS with the strange curve around it and the PRE-CUM connected by the horizontal arrow. The PS could just be a reference to the strange secret society know as the Priory of Zion, which will come into our story later. It could also have a second meaning which can be read by following the line from a position preceding P and ending in a position preceding S, thus giving us OR which is French for gold. This also satisfies the word PRE-CUM which is translated as before-with, in that we have the phrase connected with the arrow (with) and the previous letter (before). We can now update the translation of the gravestone as, 'The gold at Rennes is at Royal Reddis in the store-rooms of the fortress.

Finally we have to tackle the two outer vertical columns of letters, of which the right one is Greek and the left one Latin. The translation process here merely involves transcribing all the letters into Latin, which produces the phrase, 'ET IN ARCADIA EGO'. This is the inscription to be found on the tomb stone in Poussin's painting, 'The Shepherds of Arcadia'. Could this again be an indication that the fortress at Royal Reddis can be found in the landscape of the painting?

It is impossible to say at what stage Saunière was in his searches at any particular time and how these revelations helped him, but what is clear is that he was looking for the entrance to a crypt beneath the church and the churchyard and it is also clear that he found it. It is possible that the subterranean structure may lead to an ancient holy place, which once stood on the hill at Rennes-le-Château and which was dedicated to the Goddess Isis.

Saunière constructed a small building over the water cistern, in the graveyard, which he kept locked at all times, even when the local fire brigade needed access to the water supply to put out a fire. He and Marie Denarnaud would take long walks every day to the Bals Valley, returning with baskets full of stones, which were used to build a rock grotto in the church garden. This still stands today, but what was its purpose?

The Prosperous Priest

Around 1895, things changed beyond all recognition for Bérenger Saunière, when the priest of Rennes-le-Château became suddenly wealthy beyond all recognition. He was still receiving his meagre stipend of a few francs per month, but from this point until his death he spent the equivalent of many millions of pounds. His lifestyle became openly opulent and he began receiving visits from some of the best known celebrities of the day. Amongst the list of Saunière's distinguished guests was the opera singer Emma Calvé, Henri-Charles-Etienne Dujardin-Beaumetz, the Secretary of state for Fine Arts, who was known to be a high grade freemason and many prominent occultists. Perhaps the most remarkable caller to the court of Saunière was an individual known by the residents of the village as 'The Foreigner'. This gentleman, who called himself 'Monsieur Guillaume' was in fact John of Hapsburg, the Archduke of Austria-Hungry.

Saunière began taking long trips away from the village for around a week at a time. In the late 19th century, France had an excellent rail system and taking the early train from Montazels around 6am, it would have been possible to travel via Carcassonne and then Toulouse and be in Geneva, the North of Spain or Northern France by the late afternoon. The author followed one of Saunière's potential journeys by taking this early train in the summer of 2008, as it passed Alet-les-Bains, very early one morning and changing in the same places as Saunière would have done, ended the journey on the north coast of Spain around 5pm. It is strange to consider that the trains still run at more or less the same times and take more or less the same time to get to their destination as they did over 100 years ago.

When Jean-Luc Robin took over the running of the Saunière properties in the mid 1990's he also arranged to lease the Abbé's effects, including his private papers, diaries, documents etc. Amongst these he came across a stack of small brown pre-paid envelopes addressed to the Fritz Dorge Bank in Budapest. In Saunière's time the capital of Hungary was the major financial centre for Eastern Europe, with the same strict banking privacy laws as the Swiss banks in the west. Perhaps more importantly though Budapest was the home of the Hapsbourgs and the centre of their empire. As we have already discovered, Saunière had a close early connection with the Hapsbourgs and maybe had even been working for them to discover a secret hidden at Rennes-le-Château. If payment was being made into the Fritz Dorge bank for services rendered, then Saunière could have made the rail journey from Montazels to Budapest, to collect his remuneration, in less than 48 hours.

Confidentiality was of course extremely important to Saunière, as he could not let his superiors in the church discover his new clandestine activities and to this affect he devised a system to hide his absences from his parish. Together with the bank envelopes, Robin also discovered a collection of hand written notes saying

'My dear Brother, thank you for your letter, I have, unfortunately, been urgently called to the bedside of a sick colleague. I will reply at greater length as soon as I return. Signed: Bérenger Saunière, priest.' (Robin, Jean-Luc, *Rennes-le-Chateau, Sauniere's Secret*.)

These letters were left with Marie, to be dated appropriately, if anyone should be trying to reach him in times of his absence.

Patrice Chaplin uncovered a letter which provides further evidence of Saunière's attempts at covering up his double life. In a correspondence, sent from Spain, dated only 'Friday night', Saunière wrote;

'Dear Marie, Yesterday Guillem made a discovery that could be extraordinary if it is what I think it is, so I will have to stay here and won't be back on Sunday. Can you send the second letter to Carcassonne immediately?' (Chaplin Patrice, *City of Secrets*).

The Cathar Country

The Tour Magdela

Back at home, Saunière set about major engineering and building activities, beginning with such public spirited works as replacing the dirt track from Couiza up to Rennes-le-Château village with a properly laid road. He also had a water-tower constructed to supply running water to the entire village. After looking after his parishioners, it was time to turn his attention to the church and the land around it. He purchased six adjoining properties in the name of Marie Denarnaud to provide a space from which he was going to construct a fine domain.

No expense was to be spared and every fine detail was to be attended to. At one end of the plot two spectacular towers, with a curved connecting walkway, was constructed using the ancient city ramparts as a foundation. One of the towers, the

Tour Magdala, was developed as Saunière's library and office using beautifully crafted expensive wood-working. It was then stocked with over 1,000 books all individually bound by a professional book-binder called Henri Barrett from Toulouse, who stayed with Saunière whilst he completed this huge task.

Saunière's Library inside the Tour Magdela

The Tour Magdala is a splendid looking structure and today it provides the archetypal photograph of Rennes-le-Château. From an entrance on the curved walkway you find yourself in Saunière's library, still resplendent with the beautiful wood-working. It is easy to imagine Saunière sitting at work near the window and with the fire burning in the hearth in winter. A narrow winding staircase takes you to the turreted roof of the tower and the 360 degree panoramic views must be the most breathtaking in the Aude Valley. What is sure though is that no one would have been able to approach unnoticed from here and that the heavy metal door would have kept any intruder at bay.

A precisely laid out garden was formed beneath the walkway, complete with formal ponds and exotic animals. At the opposite end of the garden, heading toward the church, was the renovated presbytery, where Saunière and Marie Denarnaud lived and the Villa Bethania, a large flamboyant house, used to accommodate and entertain guests.

The Church of St Mary Magdalene

The Church of St Mary Magdalene at Rennes-le Château

By far the most intriguing of Saunière's renovation projects was his restoration of the Church of St. Mary Magdalene, which involved numerous highly coloured and enigmatic decorations. A cursory glance at the church reveals a Catholic Chapel albeit rather congested, but under more intensive examination the signs of a Masonic and Rosicrucian temple begin to appear from beneath the authentic veneer. A similar experience is to be had at Roslyn Chapel near Edinburgh.

Entrance tympanum

Rosicrucian Triangular style Entrance Tympanum

The central carving over the doorway reads, as if by way of a warning, 'Terribilis est locus iste'. This is a quote from Genesis chapter 28, which covers the story of Jacobs Ladder in verses 10 to 24 and translates as 'this place is terrible', with Terrible being used in the sense of awesome. The phrase is completed in the semi-circular carving directly over the door,

The Cathar Country

which reads 'Hic domus Dei est et porta coeli', *or 'This place is terrible, surely it is the house of God and this is the gate into heaven'.* (Genesis Chapter 28 verse 17)

In the story 'Jacob got up early the next morning, took the stone that was under his head and set it up as a memorial. Then he poured olive-oil on it to dedicate it to God. He named the place Beth-EL'. (Genesis Chapter 28 verse 18)

Beth-EL meaning 'house of God' is the source of the name given to Saunière's Villa Bethania. It can also be found in the New Testament story of the house of 'Bethany' in Galilee, the home of Lazarus, Martha and Mary. There is much evidence that Mary of Bethany and Mary Magdalene, the patron-saint of Rennes-le-Château to whom the church is dedicated, are one and the same person. The house in Bethany, the original Villa Bethania, contains a tomb where Lazarus was locked and from where he came back to life, or was reborn. If this account refers to a typical mystery school initiation ritual, then the association with Bethany could be a further indication of Saunière's connection to occult organisations, were the teaching of spiritual development through ritual re-birth is fundamental.

Considering Saunière's possible ritual practices, which may have involved the connection of two towers, in order to open a portal, he may have been alluding here to some sort of a Gate into Heaven, or at least a place where the veil between heaven and earth is thin? This may not be as fanciful as it originally sounds when the story of Jacobs Ladder is further examined.

'He (Jacob) rests his head on a stone. He dreamed of a stairway or ladder leading from earth into heaven, with angels ascending and descending it' (Genesis Chapter 28 verses 11/12).

The stone in the quote has often been associated with the 'Grail Stone' and in turn is symbolic of the alchemical stone or Philosopher's stone. In 'Parzival', Wolfram von Eschenbach's says...

'I will tell you how they are fed: they live from a stone whose Essence is pure...It is called lapis exilis (small, or paltry, stone). By virtue of this stone the Phoenix is burned to ashes, in which she is reborn. Thus does the Phoenix molt her feathers, after which she shines dazzling and bright, and as lovely as before. However ill a mortal man may be, from the day on which he sees the Stone, he cannot die for that week, nor does he lose his colour. For if anyone, maid or man, were to look at the grail for two hundred years, you would have to admit that his colour was as fresh as in his early prime...Such powers does the Stone confer on mortal men that their flesh and bones are soon made young again. This stone is also called the grail.' (Wolfram von Eschenbach, Parzival)

The mystery schools and other occult organisations view the Philosopher's Stone as a vital part of the process of self development, which is at the very heart of their 'Great Work'.

'In Latin it is (the Philosopher's Stone) Lapis Philosophorum. An alchemical symbol of the transmutation of humanity's lower nature into a higher, more purified spiritual state. In practical alchemy, the stone signifies the manufacturing of gold from base metal. In spiritual alchemy, it is the transmutation of the lower into the higher, a symbol of true spiritual attainment and illumination. The search for the Philosopher's stone is the search for ultimate truth and

purity'. (Cicero, Chic & Cicero, Sandra, *The Essential Golden Dawn*, pg 279)

The 'western mystery' method of training followed by occult organisations in Europe and the Americas has at its core this 'Great Work' as described by the renowned French occultist, Eliphas Levi (1801-1875). Levi trained as a priest at the very same San Sulpice in Paris, where Saunière took the parchments for translation, but he opted out of the church for a life of esoteric study. Levi wrote;

'The Great Work is, before all things, the creation of man by himself, that is to say, the full and entire consequence of his faculties and his future; it is especially the perfect emancipation of his will'. (Levi, Eliphas, *Transcendental Magic*, pg 113).

A major teaching aid in the process of the Great Work is the cabbalistic Tree of Life, which has been described by Israel Regardie as;

'A blueprint for understanding all things and relationships in the universe, including the essence of God and the soul of humanity'. (Regardie, Israel, *The Tree of Life*, pg 482).

In effect the Tree of Life and Jacobs Ladder are interchangeable and it is on these structures that an initiate would rise to a point known as the spiritual 'abyss', which they would cross to enter the area known as the 'supernal triangle', a more holy state. The next stage would be to endeavour to reach the higher spiritual realms above.

Another carving of interest in the Rosicrucian style triangular tympanum, above the church door reads, 'Domus mea domus orationis vocabitur'. This is an extract from the book of Matthew, which covers the story of Jesus in the temple, the only record in the bible of him losing his temper. The quote, which follows the scene of Jesus overturning the tables of the money changers, reads;

'My house shall be called the house of prayer'. It is interesting that Saunière did not complete the section, which ends, *'But you have made it a den of thieves'*. (Matthew 21 verse 13).

Was he using here the occult method of omission or distortion, whereby the meaning is hidden in the part reversed or turned upside-down, to refer to his covert financial dealings? The importance of this phrase, in these days of world control by financial institutions owned by a very few families, is of profound significance. Maybe this was a warning that the immoral system of usury, which was then against Jewish law and is now the corner-stone of the banking system, would one day lead to the downfall of societies. It was Paul who reminded the world that;

'The love of money was the root of all evil' and that this will lead to *'stabbing themselves all over with many pains'* (1 Timothy 6:10)

Devil and Angels

Having been gravely warned about this place of dread and awe, stepping through the door you are confronted by a hideous devil like creature, crouched beneath a scallop shaped benitier, or water stoup and a group of four brightly coloured angels. This terrifying character is generally considered to be Asmodeus the demon, who was forced by King Solomon to

The Cathar Country

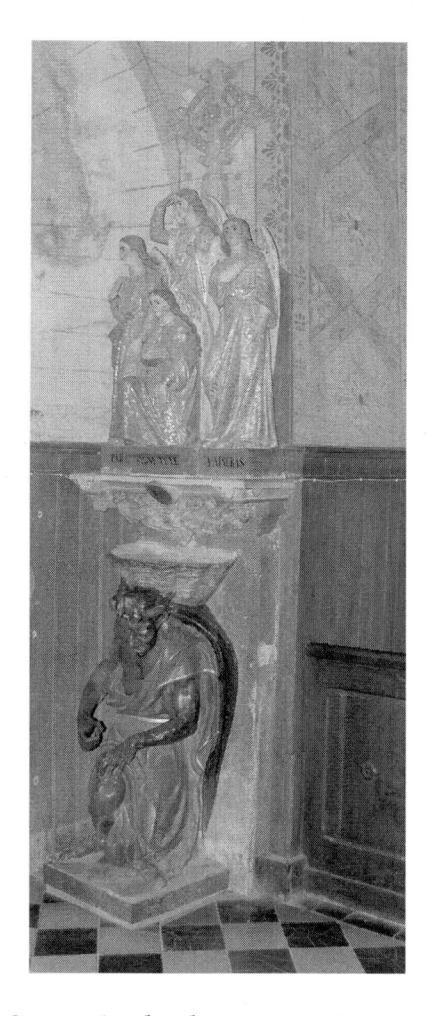

Statue in the doorway at Rennes

help him build his temple on the Temple Mount in Jerusalem. Solomon was in the possession of a magical ring, which he used to control demons, the 'one ring to rule them all' and this could well be the inspiration for Tolkien's Lord of the rings. Saunière also had such a ring with the letters BS inscribed, which he used in magical ceremonies. Strangely he had these same letters painted above the head of Asmodeus in the church, making a direct connection between the two situations. Asmodeus was also the keeper and protector of Solomon's treasure.

'Thou art Asmoday; he will not denie it, and by and by he boweth downe to the ground; he giveth the ring of venues, he absolutelie teacheth geometrie, arythmetike, astronomie, and handicrafts. To all demands he answereth fullie and trulie, he maketh a man invisible, he sheweth the places where treasure lieth, and gardeth it, if it be among the legions of Amaymon, he hath under his power seventie two legions'. (Pseudomonarchia daemonum - Johann Wier, (quoted))

The vast and elaborate structure of Solomon's Temple was constructed in 960BC and held the Ark of the Covenant and other holy treasures and secret knowledge and was destroyed by the Babylonian King Nebuchadnezzar.

'Nebuchadnezzar attacked Jerusalem again and under the leadership of his captain of the guard who burned the Temple in 586/587 BCE along with the king's house, and all the houses of Jerusalem, and every great man's house. The city wall was broken down, and the rest of the people that were left in the city, and the fugitives that fell away to the king of Babylon, with the remnant of the multitude, were carried away'. (2 Kings verse 25).

The Cathar Country

Asmodeus or Rex Mundi

The temple was reconstructed in 516BC but met its fate in 70AD, when it was destroyed by the Romans, who removed the temple treasure to Rome. Rome was in turn conquered by the Visigothic King Aleric I, in an attack which lasted six days. The vast wealth that had been brought to Rome over the centuries, from throughout the empire was carried out of the city on chariots, following the Visigothic army. This booty, which would have included the treasures of the temple, made its way to the stronghold of Carcassonne, were it stayed until the Meroviginian King Clovis forced the Visigoths south with their treasure to Rheddae. Today as the village of Rennes-le-

Château, the signs of the old city of Rheddae are still seen around the mountainside beneath the village, but the treasures are considered lost. Or is Asmodeus still protecting it somewhere either in the vicinity of the church, or on the surrounding countryside?

Neil on the Devil's Armchair

Sitting at the side of a long winding path, on a mountain near the town of Rennes-les-Bains, there is a carved boulder called the 'Le Fauteuil du Diable', or the Devil's Armchair, which appears to be a perfect fit for the strangely distorted statue of Asmodeus in the church. Next to this megalith is a small circular spring called the 'Source du Cercle' or 'Source of the Circle'. Could it be that the circle our Asmodeus is indicating with his fingers is intended to lead the seeker to this place and could it be that if he was to sit on his armchair he would be looking in the direction of something secreted on the mountainside? The Devil's Armchair faces east so it is

The Cathar Country

possible that our Demon was signifying the ancient sacred practice of watching the sunrise. Today the mountainside is covered by trees, but it is still possible to see that in-fact Le Fauteuil du Diable, is facing the holy mountain of Cardou.

Source du Cercle

The initials BS, above the demon's head has been the source of much debate, does it relate to Saunière and his collaborator, Boudet or was Bérenger Saunière showing an unusually high degree of self obsession by signing his own work? Or are we again being directed to the beautiful Languedoc countryside and a valley not far from the Devil's Armchair and the Source du Cercle, where the two rivers of the Blanque and Sals join to form a natural, if gentle 'water stoup'.

The meeting of the Rivers Blanque and Sals

The research of Marilyn, Simmans and Wallace-Murphy into the bloodline of the high priests of the Jerusalem temple has produced a family line called 'Rex Deus', who trace their decedancy back through the line of Jesus. This royal family of Israel are said to have fled, after the crucifixion of Jesus, to avoid Roman reprisals and were to become the leading families of the Languedoc and to have settled in various parts of Europe, including Champaign and Gisors.

It is said that James the son of Jesus came over to Britain with Joseph of Arimathea, but during the Dark Ages, traces of the families become murky. After the Norman Conquest history tells of how the long-reigning King Malcolm Canmore (1030-1093) of Scotland took the Saxon Princess Margaret as his wife. Margaret was not only the exiled true pretender to the throne

The Cathar Country

of England; she was also of the Davidic line of Israel and a member of Rex Deus. On her journey back to Britain from asylum in Hungary, Margaret was protected by two knights, who would have also been of the Rex Deus line. These escorts were awarded lands in Scotland and their descendants have become amongst the leading families, the Leslie and the St. Clair clans.

From tracing the Rex Deus families to their adopted homes, it is clear that the Knights Templar, the powerful order of warrior monks, were not only intimately connected to the line of Israel but can be said to be direct descendants. After beginning life in the courts of the Count of Champagne, the Templars quickly moved to Israel, where they took up residency on the Temple Mount; they had gone home. It is noteworthy that Rex-Deus, which translates as 'King-God', were, like Asmo-Deus the 'King-Demon', in the business of protecting the treasures of Solomon's Temple and that both have a direct connection with the church of St. Mary Magdalene at Rennes-le-Château.

In the Jewish teaching of the Cabbala, Asmodeus is also known as 'Samual the Back', the negative ruler of 'Geburah', the concept of justice. It is clear that he would not be a welcome adversary, so the painted letters above the demon's head and directly below the angels, provide something of a remedy. The usual form of this phrase is 'Par ce signe tu vaincras', 'by this sign shalt thou conquer', but Saunière, in his usual enigmatic way, added the word 'le' the result being 'Par ce signe tu le vaincras', or 'by this sign shalt thou conquer HIM'.

The angels of Geburah, the opponents of Asmodeus are the;

'Seraphim, or the spirits of burning with zeal', (Mathers, MacGregor (translated), *The Key of Solomon the King,* pg 122)

So it could well be that the four garishly painted angels on the statue, which are indicating the sign of the cross, are the ones to which the carving refers.

True to the theme of Saunière's domain, behind the apparent Catholic Christian appearance of the statue, there are hidden occult meanings. The addition of the extra two letters to the painted phrase increase the number of letters to 22, which is extremely important Cabbalisticly, as this is the number of letters in the Hebrew alphabet. Each Hebrew letter represents amongst other things, an aspect of consciousness as well as numbers. It may also be relevant that the new letters appear in positions 13 and 14, this being the date when the Knights Templar Grand Master, Jacques Molay, was burned alive in 1314.

Of greater importance though is that the four elements of alchemy are quite clearly shown in the statue; the devil as Rex Mundi is the Lord of the EARTH, above him is the WATER stoup followed by the Salamanders, representing FIRE and the angels are AIR. The four elements represent the four letters of the Tetragrammaton, YHWH, the holy name of God, which has become pronounceable in English, as Yahway or Jehovah. The statue is constructed to follow the progression up the Cabalistic Tree of Life, beginning with earth at the bottom and rising to the angels, representing the holy realms at the top of the tree. Above this a Rosicrucian style cross brings the further element of Spirit into the equation representing the areas above the tree. This would now provide the five elements needed to construct a pentagram, the geometric figure which represents Venus and the Magdalene and which can be found in the natural landscape around Rennes-le-Château. (See chapter 7.)

Again from a cabbalistic perspective, the Hebrew letter representing this fifth element of spirit goes by the name of 'Shin' and to add this to the original Tetragrammaton (YHWH), would produce a new holy word, which represents the Christ Force. The whole statue therefore, whilst appearing on the surface to represent some quite contradictory separate elements, appears to represent the same concept as Jesus when taken in its entirety.

The fresco of Jesus, the Sals valley and the Bas-reliefs of Mary

Having conquered your demon and crossed the threshold of the church you are confronted with an overcrowded space, packed with colour and a Masonic and Rosicrucian, black and white chequered floor. The detail in the church is, possibly intentionally, overwhelming and far too much to take in.

On entering, the left hand wall above the confessional is dominated by a haut-relief fresco depicting the Sermon on the Mount, but with some interesting additions. On the bottom right hand of the flat painted background, the carved wooden pulpit support pillar, where the parchments were said to have been found, can clearly be seen disregarded on a rock-pile. Above this an elderly figure makes his or her way, with the help of what appears to be an umbrella, towards an overgrown area, or bush. This figure could be Marie

Dénarnaud, or Saunière's friend Boudet or possible Bigou, fleeing to the border.

Bas-relief fresco of the 'Sermon on the Mount'

The words 'VENEZ À MOI, VOUS TOUS QUI SOUFFREZ ET QUI ÊTES ACCABLES, ET JE VOUS SOULAGERAI', painted below the scene, translates as 'come to me, all who suffer, and I will relieve your pain'. This is a quote from the Sermon on the Mount as told by Bernard of Clairvaux in his work, 'Dialogue d'un juste avec Dieu', or 'Dialogue of a righteous man with God'. The original quote is from Matthew 11:28, and reads 'Come to me, all you who are weary and burdened, and I will give you rest'. St. Bernard was the most influential member of the Cistercian movement and was a close associate of the Count of Champaign at the time when the Knights Templar were instigated at his court near Troyes. He was responsible for gaining papal legitimacy for the Templars at the Council of Troyes in 1128. The Cistercians may therefore be seen as the religious non-combative side of the Templar

The Cathar Country

Order. The association with the Knights Templar and Rennes-le-Château through the Blancheforts, whose family chapel the church used to be, is well documented and maybe Saunière wanted to bring the importance of this connection to the attention of future visitors.

In the scene the gathered on-lookers on the hill-side below Jesus are paying no attention to the bag of gold nuggets shown split open below them, taking a centre stage position. Is Saunière suggesting that gold is to be found on the hillsides nearby, or is he showing the mystery teaching of spiritual alchemy, that it is more profitable to seek spiritual gold than earthy treasures, or is there a further hidden meaning to be sought?

In his film 'Henry Lincoln's Guide to Rennes-le-Chateau and the Aude Valley', Lincoln pointed to the similarities between the scene in the fresco and the landscape surrounding Rennes-le-Château. Jesus is standing on a small pointed hill, with flowers scattered around the slopes. This hill resembles a comparable mound called Roque Fumade, which used to be owned by the fleure (or Flower) family. To the left a hill top village resembles Rennes-le-Château and to the right the ruined castle is in a position indicative of Caustaussa.

Was Saunière directing our attention to treasure hidden on Roque Fumade, or is their still more to the story? The fresco of Jesus is facing another bas-relief on the altar right through the church, where Mary Magdalene sits in a cave with the ruins of a castle and a mountain visible through the cave opening. This distant view from the cave is thought to have been painted by Saunière himself and that it represents Mount Cardou and Caustaussa Castle. From his place on Roque

Fumade on the fresco, Jesus is actually looking right down the valley of the River Sals, along what is now the road D613, past Caustaussa, Blanchfort, Mount Cardou and to Arque, where a small cave can be found on the side of the road, just through the village.

Altar fresco of Mary Magdalene

Early traditions in the South of France, dating back through the Dark Ages, tell of how Mary Magdalene fled to the area, landing at Marseille and living in a cave in the mountains. Whether this is the cave where she lived or not, it is still used as a meeting place for individuals and groups interested in the Magdalene, the Dark Madonna and the goddess archetype of

Isis. Remarkably the cave stands at the intersection of the planes of the natural pentagram, found in the surrounding landscape. As a side note, it is of interest that the name of Marie de Negre de Blanchefort who is central to the whole story of Saunière and Rennes-le-Château and who has been connected to the Magdalene, translates as 'Black Marie of the White Fort'. Saunière's chess game plays on.

Cave of Mary Magdelene

Another interpretation of the geography of the fresco is suggested by the author. In order for the hill on which Jesus stands to be Roque Fumade, there would have been a large amount of artistic licence used, as Fumade lies behind Rennes-le-Château and Caustaussa and not in the foreground as depicted. An alternative theory would suggest that the small pointed mountain in the left background, to the right of the hill top village, is in-fact Roque Fumade and that the scene of Jesus with his followers is set on Mount Cardou. This would correct the geography with the whole of the scene in the fresco and would have the result of drawing attention to the ancient holy mountain. This would also put right the problems of perspective and place Rennes, Caustaussa and the cave in the correct positions relative to each other.

Jesus in the haut-relief, is not just wearing the traditional white robe, but is depicted with an additional red cloak, with gold stitching. This unusual choice of clothing, which is also shown in the statue of Jesus and John the Baptist on the wall to the right, opposite the entrance, indicates a royal bloodline, much in the same way as does a red-carpet. These symbols of power are still used today to signify certain royal lineages, under the generic title of 'Sacrae Coronae Regni'.

Many researchers, particularly since the discovery of the Dead Sea Scrolls in Qumran near Jerusalem in 1947, have made a connection between John the Baptist, Jesus, and Jesus' brother James. Knight and Lomas, have describing them all as;

'Senior members of the Essene group, who lived in a cave community above the Dead Sea until around AD 68'. (Knight, Christopher & Lomas, Robert, *The Hiram Key*).

This group is thought to have consisted of the elite priestly families who ran the Temple on the Mount and whose bloodline continues today.

The Church Statues

The two statues and the two babies

There are eight other statues decorating the church, evenly set out in four sets of parallel rows along the walls. Each one equally brightly coloured and each one a little oversized for its interior space. Saunière had big ideas and now existed in a larger world, but even he could not turn a once family chapel into a cathedral.

Behind the altar with the bas-relief of Mary Magdalene are statues of Mary and Joseph, suspended from the wall facing each other under a half domed ceiling, painted in the Egyptian style, blue starry sky reminiscent of those dedicated to the Goddess Maat. As is to be expected Mary is holding the infant Jesus, but curiously so is Joseph. This second child may be

James the Just, brother of Jesus and leader of the early church after his death. An alternative identification for this infant is Thomas Didymus (both Thomas and Didymus mean 'twin'), who since the study of the Gospel of Thomas and the Book of Thomas, discovered in the deserts of Nag Hammadi, on the Egyptian banks of the Nile, in December 1945, has been thought to have been the twin of Jesus.

Just in front of the altar is a tall three layer statue of St. Anthony of Padua, the patron saint of lost things, who considering Saunière's background of searching, both physically and esoterically, deserves his prime position. St Anthony is being held up by four angels; possibly the same Seraphim, or the spirits of burning with zeal, which are keeping Asmodeus at bay near the door. Unseen to everyone but the priest, one of the angels is baring one knee, very much in the way of a Masonic initiate. Could this be further evidence of Saunière's Rosicrucian connections?

Looking at Anthony of Padua, diagonally across the church is the saint's name sake, St Anthony the Hermit. On the spectacular Gorge of Galimus, cutting it's way in the 300 metre deep ravine of the Agly River and clinging onto the sheer cliff around 18 miles from Rennes is the Hermitage of St Anthony. Whether or not Saunière was pointing us to this place by including the statue in his church, we may never know, but what is without a doubt, is that no visit to the area would be complete without a visit to this stunning, yet peaceful holy place. At the end of the Gorge, is the town of Saint Paul de Fenouillet, where the road and shop signs have a Spanish element to them and it is here that the Abbé Bigou crossed the border, fleeing the French anti-clerical guillotine in 1792, taking so many secrets with him.

The Cathar Country

Hermitage of St Antony, on the Gorge of Galimus

Saunière's statue tricks may have stretched to their very positioning within the church. If a line is traced from the statue of St. Germaine to St. Roch to St. Anthony the Hermit, to St. Anthony of Padua to St.Luke, a giant letter 'M' is created around the statue of Mary Magdalene and taking the initials of the saints starting again from Germaine, the word GRAAL is spelt out; the French word for Grail.

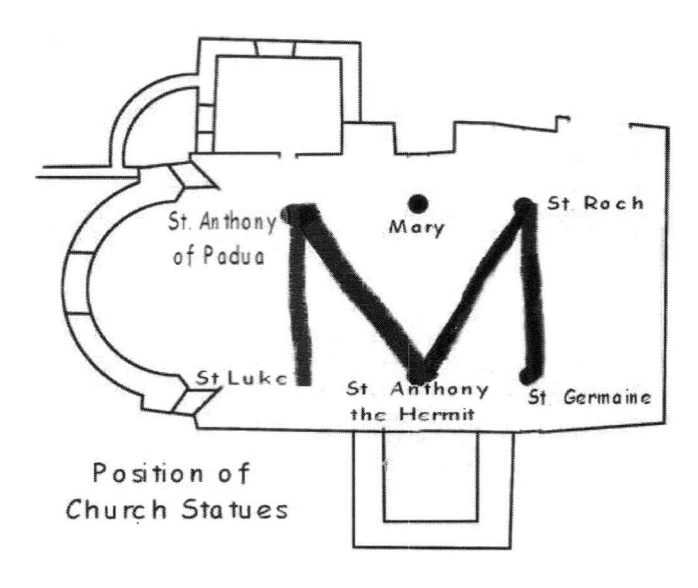

[Diagram: Floor plan of church showing position of statues — St. Anthony of Padua, Mary, St. Roch, St. Luke, St. Anthony the Hermit, St. Germaine — with a large 'M' drawn over them. Labeled "Position of Church Statues"]

The Church Statues forming an 'M' around the Statue of Mary. Also spelling the word GRAAL (grail) in reverse.

Stations of the Cross

The story of Christ's journey to his execution is generally recorded in catholic churches in the Stations of the Cross; displayed in varying sophistication, from simple numbers to elaborate and detailed bas-reliefs, spaced out around the walls. In the church of Mary Magdalene, Saunière did not miss the opportunity to add more colour to his confusing display, with a row of highly decorated and slightly oversized plaques. He also remained true to form by painting in various extra details, which have been the source of much study, speculation and theorizing. It is possible that some of Saunière's hidden messages may never be picked up, but there

The Cathar Country

are three in particular, that have produced much conjecture and theorizing;

Station VI may provide a particularly complex message, initially suggested by Henry Lincoln and which appears to point to a particular place in the countryside viewable from the churchyard. In the left background a Roman centurion is holding a 'high shield', or 'Haut Bouclier', but it may be important that the same feature can also be found in the church at Rocamadour. The phrase could be pronounced 'Au Bout Clier', meaning 'at the bottom of the enclosure', if using the old word French 'Clier' for enclosure. The shield in the art work covers half of a tower, producing 'half tower', or 'demi tour', which could also mean 'a half turn'.

The woman in the foreground handing the cloth to Jesus is Veronica, or 'Veronica with the cloth', or 'Veronica au lin'. It is thought that this may be directing us towards Mount Cardou, a china clay mountain or a mountain of kaolin. The complex wordplay here involves, Veronica with the cloth being changed to 'vers haut nid kaolin', or 'towards the high china clay peak'. Finally we have Simon of Cyrene, the man standing behind Jesus, who in the biblical story helped him to carry his cross. From this we get 'Simon regarde', or 'Simon is looking', which can be read as 'cime on regarde', or 'the crest one is looking at'.

So putting all this together we have; 'at the bottom of the enclosure, make a half turn towards Cardou. One is looking at the crest'. Following these instructions from the church cemetery you will, in fact end up looking at Cardou and just in front of the great mountain you will see the crest of Blanchefort, the location of the Templar observation point, built under the Grand Master-ship of Bertrand de Blanchefort, the previous owner of the church.

Stations of the Cross – VI – VIII - XIV

Station VIII could be hiding another interesting meaning. The woman in the scene is veiled as if in mourning and holds a child with a blue Scottish tartan cloth. This could relate to Scottish Rite Freemasonry, whose members refer to themselves as 'children of the widow', in reference to the story of Hiram Abiff, which is acted out during the Masonic third degree of initiation, known as one of the blue degrees.

Station XIV shows what is probably the most contentious hidden message, introduced to the scene in the simplest of manners. Station XIV usually depicts Jesus being placed into the tomb by Joseph of Arimathea, a process described in the gospel of Matthew;

'When evening had come, a rich man from Arimathaea, named Joseph, who himself was also Jesus' disciple came. This man went to Pilate, and asked for Jesus' body. Then Pilate commanded the body to be given up. Joseph took the body, and wrapped it in a clean linen cloth, and laid it in his own new tomb, which he had hewn out in the rock, and he rolled a great stone to the door of the tomb, and departed. Mary Magdalene was there, and the other Mary, sitting opposite the tomb'. (Matt 27:57).

Under normal circumstances a ceremony using burial spices would have been preformed, but in the case of the crucifixion of Jesus, time was an important factor. Under Jewish law no work could be carried out on the Sabbath, which was due to start at 6pm and this included the burial processes. Therefore the placing of Jesus into the tomb is generally thought of as being rushed, with the intention of returning after the Sabbath to complete the usual burial ceremonies. But Saunière has painted a moon in the sky, posing the question as to whether Jesus was being removed from the tomb later that night and not being placed there in the late afternoon.

A Hidden Room

During Saunière's excavating activities in the church graveyard it was said that he could be seen to go into his sacristy and appear in the churchyard. The sacristy is the priest's changing room, which at Rennes is entered through a door next to the statue of St. Anthony of Padua, in front of the altar. At first examination the room appears innocent enough with a bench, some assorted items of furniture, including a provincial chest of drawers and built in wardrobe and it is here that you find the secret to Saunière's miraculous appearance in the churchyard. An examination of the wardrobe reveals a hidden door to the back, which would have been extremely difficult to discover when it was full of priestly garments. Beyond this door is a small room with an external curved wall with a tiny circular window, which can be seen from the outside.

Circular hidden room at Rennes-le-Château church

Jean-Luc Robin tells of how a team of American researchers conducted a sounding examination in the interior of the church in 2002 and that they concluded, without doubt that a vaulted chamber was present beneath the flooring. Speaking at a conference in Saunière's garden, of the results of this inspection, the architect Paul Saussez concluded that the secret room behind the sacristy once contained an entrance to the crypt and that another opening existed in the churchyard.

This would explain the mystery of Saunière's strange appearances outside the church.

Conflict with the Bishop

As the end of the 19th centaury drew near, Saunière was spending his unexplained wealth as freely as royalty and he had developed tastes to match, which he shared with a procession of VIP guests. On 6th June 1897 he held a lavish banquet for his friend Mgr Billard, bishop of Carcassonne, by way of an official launch for his new church improvements. Amongst the items on the menu they enjoyed; a whole list of entrées, including foie gras, lobster and an assortment of shellfish and fish dishes, three roasts, a dozen desserts, fine wines, a cask of fine wines and with Havana cigars to complete the feast.

Then things changed in December 1901, when the Bishop Billard died and was replaced by Mgr Paul-Felix Beurain de Beausejour as the new bishop of Carcassonne. This elder churchman was not going to accept Saunière's cover story of donations from wealthy anonymous benefactors and more than this he was determined to discipline this wayward priest and bring him under his control, with a continuing campaign bordering on obsession.

After trying to catch out Saunière through his accounting, Beausejour finally ran out of tolerance and in 1909, he ordered Saunière to take up the post of priest of the tiny hamlet of Coustouge and appointed the Abbé Marty to the position of Curate of Rennes-le-Château, to replace him. Saunière refused the move out right, telling the bishop;

'I declare to you, Monseigneur, with all the firmness of a respectful son; no, I will not go'. (de Sede, Gerard, *Rennes-le-Château.* P53).

This was of course an extremely bold reply to his immediate superior, but he had the support of his parishioners at Rennes, with whom he had been extremely generous throughout his years of wealth. The mayor of the village also proved supportive and wrote to the bishop explaining quite succinctly, that the presbytery would not be made available to the new Abbé, that there was no free accommodation for him to rent in the village and that unofficial church services would be carried out by the Abbé Saunière in his conservatory chapel, connected to the Villa Bethania.

Saunière's conservatory chapel

The Cathar Country

The bishop was not going to take this insubordinate rebuff without a fight and brought Saunière before a hearing of the Ecclesiastic Tribunal of the Diocese, under the charge of trafficking in masses, which was the only offence he could put together, faced with a wall of silence from all at Rennes-le-Château. It is clear, from Saunière's accounts that he did perform some masses for the amount of one franc each, but to make his massive income, he would have been performing masses for many years after his death. It is also the case that putting income from other sources down to the performing of masses would have been an ingenious way of laundering it.

The case took place on 5th November 1910 and not surprisingly it was held that the charges were 'not sufficient nor judicially established', but in an attempt to placate the bishop, Saunière was sentenced to ten days at the monastery of Prouilhe, which he managed to serve with a few of his friends, who had also fallen foul of the church authorities. During his enforced break, Saunière wrote to his housekeeper Marie, of the blandness of the food available at the monastery, but thanking her for the bottles of her liqueur, which he was taking a few glasses of each evening. He signed the letter 'your affectionate Bérenger', which would appear unusually informal for an employer.

On returning home and with counter attack on his mind Saunière approached the Vatican direct in an attempt to have his priestly duties restored. He employed a two point strategy, which included an astounding declaration of poverty and the appointing of a highly experienced legal representative, by the name of Canon Huguet from Agen.

As the process in Rome was taking its course, the bishop Beausejour declared Saunière 'suspans a divinis', which removed his right to carry out ceremonial priestly duties. The bishop also printed an ordered for Saunière to repay back all 'illegally acquired amounts', in a local religious publication. Maybe the bishop was getting desperate, because this was an unwise act, as the previous Ecclesiastic hearing had held that nothing had been proved. Therefore no illegally received amounts existed and to imply that there was, was at least bordering on libel. Saunière passed this message onto the bishop through his new lawyer, mentioning a new law suite, this time in the law courts and looking for damages.

The outcome from Mgr Giorgi, the secretary to the Vatican council was that it should be a matter of conscience for the Abbé and that the bishop was guilty of an abuse of power. Also the charges levied against Saunière were against canon law. The Bishop was still not prepared to give up and in 1915, published a declaration that the restrictions placed on Saunière's priestly duties, remained in force, despite the Vatican decision. In response to this the Vatican made a pronouncement that all restrictions placed on Saunière by the bishop were annulled. It would probably have been better for bishop Beausejour if he had been aware of Saunière's highly placed friends before he had embarked on his lengthy power battle with the priest.

The fairytale in decline

Although Saunière had won his tit-for-tat battle with bishop Beausejour, the whole thing had taken its toll on our priest and his health had begun to decline. He took a last trip to

The Cathar Country

Lourdes, hoping for an answer to his growing problems of gout and cirrhosis, no doubt brought on by his ostentatious life-style, but the great days of flamboyance had all but ended and Saunière was becoming increasingly introverted.

Then in 1914 the outbreak of the First World War was to seriously affect travel within Europe and this had the additional consequence of isolating some of the banks Saunière was using to manage his cash flow. Records show that at this time, some of Saunière's creditors were not getting paid, which goes some way to prove that he was either using foreign banks to look after his cash or he was getting paid through these organisations.

Visitors were now rare at Rennes-le-Château and Saunière had become increasingly solitary as his health declined. Then on the bitter cold evening of 17th January 1917, after leaving a blazing fire in the Tour Magdala, where he had spent the afternoon working and enjoying a few glasses of wine, he collapsed on the walkway with what was probably a stroke. It was around an hour later when Marie found him after realising that he had not returned for supper and with the help of a couple of strong villagers he was carried to his bed in a coma. He recovered briefly the next day, but our curé must have realised that he was on borrowed time as he instructed Marie to burn certain papers from a drawer in his desk. All Saunière's belongings, buildings and cash were already in Marie's name and it is said that she was fully informed of all his secrets, so Sauniere could have felt that all his affairs were in order, apart perhaps from making his peace with his God.

For Saunière this may have been his most formidable task and he wanted the job done properly. He chose not to call for a friend who may have let him off lightly but instead, on the 21st January he asked for the Abbé Rivière, of Esperaza, whom he did not like on a personal level, but respected for his faith. Rivière spent a whole afternoon listening to Saunière's final confession and appeared to be visibly shaking when he left, after refusing to perform the last rites.

Whatever Saunière told Rivière, it had a serious and debilitating effect on the priest and it is said that his personality changed from a jovial disposition to one of introversion, to the extent of being totally withdrawn. He also changed some of the decorations in his church, including the addition of a Christ figure in a grotto, built out of the same stone from the near-by mountains, as Saunière's Lourdes Grotto. The figure is lying on a shroud but not covered by it, indicating that this Christ figure could still be alive, whilst in his burial shroud. A reference has to be made here with number XIV of the Stations of the Cross at Rennes-le-Château, which shows the figure of Jesus possibly being removed from the tomb, probably soon after burial.

The following morning, the 22nd January, Saunière passed away as the sun rose over the horizon. The funeral service took place in Saunière's beloved church on the 24th January and was performed by three priests, a highly unusually situation for a mere village priest. The Abbé Riviere, having had time to absorb whatever Saunière had revealed to him, performed the last rites and he was laid to rest in the churchyard, which had been such a place of controversy, intrigue and discovery for him. Marie was heartbroken and she remained in the churchyard long after the funeral was completed and visited the grave every evening. Marie and Saunière had shared an amazing whirlwind, fairytale lifetime together and now she was left alone with a secret, 'advantages of which even kings would have great pains to draw' and for which people had died and which had produced untold riches.

Marie stayed on in the presbytery, living off produce from the garden and orchard and her small collection of hens and ducks. She was now responsible for the whole of Saunière's domain, but cash flow appears to have all but dried up and she started taking in lodgers to help to keep things going and to pay the huge land taxes. She did not mix with the villagers much and now that the stream of visitors had ceased to run to the door, it must have been a lonely life.

The First World War ended and the Second World War began and still Marie was living alone and visiting the grave of 'our dear departed' faithfully every day. She had been forced to put the whole domain up for sale, but had turned down the many offers she had received, as she just could not face leaving the memories of Saunière and the good days. In 1923, she wrote to a friend:

'As you can guess, all summer long I've had people wanting to buy the place, but I just can't bring myself to do it. At the last moment, I always back off. Everything is too full of memories of our dear departed. I just can't bear to give it all up and I keep putting off a decision'. (Robin, Jean-Luc, *Rennes-le-Chateau, Sauniere's Secret*. Pg177)

The house was being used as a base for the local resistance movement, when a business man from Perpignan by the name of Noel Corbu made contact, with a view to purchasing the whole of the property. Marie was again reluctant to reach a deal, but in time she became friends with Noel and his family and eventually an agreement was reached that would suit all concerned. Marie would remain the owner of the property for the rest of her life and leave everything to Noel in her will, which was completed in July 1946. They would all live together in the domain, the family in the house and Marie in the presbytery and in that way Marie would keep her memories close and would have the company of a family. The dangers of such an arrangement are all too plain to comprehend, but in the case of the Corbus and Mademoiselle Marie Dénarnaud, this was the perfect arrangement and for Marie. It provided a wonderful new lease of life.

Noel Corbu's daughter, Clair in her book written with Antoine Captier spoke of these early days after moving in with Marie:

'Mademoiselle Marie, as we called her, was already seventy eight years old when we came to live with her. She was a little woman, one could say tiny and rather bent. The years had wrinkled her face, without dimming the mischievous glint in her eye. Rheumatism had knotted and deformed her hands, which sometimes gave her a lot of pain.

Like all our old village peasant women, she dressed constantly in dark colours with her eternal – sometimes grubby – apron tied round her waist and a scarf round her head.

She'd been used to living on her own for such a long time that she preferred to continue living in the presbytery, rather than coming to join us in the Villa Bethania. She spent most of the time in her kitchen, a gloomy little room with smoke blackened walls. A couple of slow-burning logs smouldering on the fire, keeping beans or soup

The Cathar Country

for ever simmering in a "toupi", in the best peasant tradition. She was a marvellous cook and her jugged rabbit was beyond compare. In a little building opposite the presbytery and adjoining the villa, she kept a few rabbits which had burrowed right through to the earth. And she had a dozen chickens and a few ducks.

Despite her great age, she was still very alert; hardly a day passed without her going out into the countryside to collect grass for the rabbits or to gather a bundle of kindling for the fire. In the evening, she loved to come and chat with us for a while, particularly with my father, whom she greatly admired. However, if he questioned her about the story of the Abbé Saunière, she would never give him a direct answer – but would unfailingly demonstrate a disconcerting talent for changing the subject'. (Captier Antoine & Corbu Claire, L'Heritage De L'Abbe Sauniere - Rennes-Le-Château).

She told Corbu many times of a great secret that would one day make him rich and that she would pass it on to him before she died. She would speak of great riches that the people of Rennes-le-Château were walking upon without knowing it.

As her health began to get the better of her, Marie eventually moved into the Villa Bethania with the Corbu family, to be more closely looked after. She suffered a severe stroke on 24th January 1953 and was unable to speak; she was also paralysed from the attack and died five days later without recovering. She had been unable to pass on any secrets, no matter what they were and it could be that the last person, who knew the whole secret of Bérenger Saunière and Rennes-le-Château and maybe even the ancient secrets of the Blanchefort dynasty, had left this reality.

The Mystery Continues

With the loss of both Bérenger Saunière and Marie Dénarnaud we have no true witnesses to the events at Rennes-le-Château left, but the mystery has not died. On the contrary it has grown over the years as untold numbers of researchers have added to the body of knowledge surrounding these fascinating events. The sheer wealth of books and websites covering the subject matter is overwhelming, but neither the story nor this beautiful area of Southern France belongs to any single person or organisation.

If the answers are to be uncovered it is going to have to be from the work of many, looking at the subject matter from various directions. But please take a warning from the author; do not put a toe into the mystery of Rennes-le-Château, unless you are ready to be swept up in a study which will take you in many unexpected directions; some can be disconcerting, but all will be fascinating. As the prolific Rennes-le-Château researcher, Lionel Fanthorpe once said; 'it is like peeling an onion from the inside'.

The Saunière mystery lives on today, but it seems to have created more questions than answers. Was he rewarded by the Hapsburgs for services rendered? Was he paid off by the church for keeping certain secrets? Was he a powerful alchemical magician that produced gold from the rocks of Mount Cardou? Did he find the ancient treasure of the Visigoths or the Cathars, or is their something more astounding, yet to be uncovered? Only time will tell.

Chapter 5

January 17th, Priests, Players and Post-Mortems

The strange matter of the 17th January in the story of Bérenger Sauniére and Rennes-le-Château is somewhat of a side issue to the main narrative of the sudden appearance of the priest's apparently unlimited wealth, as are the unexpected deaths which seem to afflict people closely associated to the mystery. A single occurrence of these events would not be note worthy, whereas two similar events could be put down as a coincidence, but after a number of repeated similar incidents a point is arrived at, when the situation can well be referred to as a mystery.

17th January

The first occurrence of the seemingly insignificant date 17th January, is the date of the death of the Marie d'Hautpoul de Blanchefort, the last member of the Hautpoul de Blanchefort dynasty of Rennes-le-Château, to hold the family secret until she died in 1781. The coded parchments, which are said to have been hidden by the Abbé Antoine Bigou in the church of Mary Magdalene, were discovered by Saunière and taken for decoding to St. Sulpice in Paris, whose feast day is 17th January.

After gaining the decipherment of the parchments and becoming massively wealthy, Saunière decorated his church and placed a statue of St. Anthony the Hermit in a central position facing Mary Magdalene, the patron saint of the church. Again the feast day of St. Anthony is 17th January and it is also the date of his death. Another feature, which used to happen every 17th January in the church at Rennes, was the phenomenon known as the 'blue apples'; a light display, that would appear through a stained glass window at mid day and move along the wall. Unfortunately the mayor of Rennes-le-Château had the small circular shaft in the wall, which used to let in the light for this display, filled in whilst re-pointing the exterior walls.

Much speculation has been made as to the possible connection of the blue apples light display with the translation of the Shepherdess Parchment;

'Shepherdess no temptation. That Poussin (&) Teniers hold the key. Peace 681. By the cross and this horse of God, I complete this guardian daemon at midday. Blue apples'.

Maybe it was also this connection, which led Saunière to purchase the Teniers painting 'St. Anthony and St. Paul in the Desert', an art work which brings to mind St. Anthony's Hermitage, on the Languedoc's Gorge de Galimus.

Probably the most remarkable instance of the date 17th January is to be found in the church yard in Rennes-les-Bains, where the priest Henri Boudet has altered the gravestone of his predecessor, Jean Vie.

Grave of Jean Vie

The grave lies in a specific position to mark out an alignment from the pointer on the top of the iron cross above the grave stone, through a globe above the church, then through a megalith on the hillside beyond and eventually ending at Rennes-le-Château, probably to indicate the position of the grave of Marie de Blanchefort. The name 'Jean Vie' can be pronounced in the same way as 'Janvier', or 'January' and towards the bottom of the stone, two numbers have been carved to emphasised the 1 and the 7. Thus we are led again to January 17th.

The Abby Bérenger Sauniere Rennes-le-Château

During his time as priest, Bérenger Saunière had two great companions, Henri Boudet, the priest of Rennes-les-Bains and Antoine Gellis, the priest of Caustaussa, both neighbouring parishes to Rennes-le-Château. All three of the friends became wealthy and it is highly likely that they were all parties to the legendary secret. But these conspirators have, in their turn, added to the legend by meeting an end under questionable circumstances.

The Abbé Bérenger Saunière suffered a stroke on the evening of January 17th 1917 on his way back to his presbytery, having spent the whole afternoon working in the library in the Tour Magdala. It is said that during this time, Saunière received two strange and sinister guests, who left as silently as they arrived. Although he recovered from his coma for a short while, Saunière died five days later on the 22nd January, but was it the plan of the unusual guests to assassinate him on the 17th?

Soon after he had passed away, Saunière was positioned in an armchair, whilst a whole stream of visitors filed passed him and plucked a red pom-pom from his shawl, in a strange ritual of remembrance. Some accounts of this ceremony have the villagers filing passed, but some tell of strangers arriving in the village, taking part and quickly leaving. Some stories also say that Mary Dénarnaud had ordered Saunière's coffin five days before he collapsed, from a carpenter from Couiza, by the name of Bousgarbies, which would suggest prior knowledge of the stroke on the 17th. There is no evidence of this and the receipt from the carpenter was only dated when the bill was paid on the 12th June 1917. From the actions of Marie over the many years she spent with Saunière, it is utterly impossible to consider that she could have ever meant him any harm. But then we don't know the secret or what it might have required from its holders.

The Abbé Henri Boudet
Rennes-Les-Bains

Henri Boudet was born in Quillan, just down the valley from Rennes, in the year 1861. Recognised early in his childhood of being of high intellect, he was destined for the priesthood and arrived as priest of Rennes-les-Bains in November 1837. Many have speculated on the role of Boudet, suggesting that he may have acted as the low profile force driving Saunière's outward activities, just as Rennes-les-Bains hides in the Aude valley surrounded by mountains, whilst Rennes-le-Château stands high above for all to see.

Boudet combined a love of the archaeology of the area, with a degree in English in authoring the book, 'The True Celtic Language and the Cromlech of Rennes-les-Bains'. On first appearance this book, which ostensibly attempts to prove that the English language was the forerunner for all other world languages, is at least eccentric if not utterly insane. But it appears that Boudet had employed similar encoding techniques as Johnathan Swift, the author of 'Gulliver's Travels', who published a highly complicated encrypted work called 'Disclosure in Proof of the Antiquity of the English Language, showing by various Examples that Hebrew, Greek and Latin have been derived from English'. No one has every successfully extracted the full meaning of Boudet's strange volume, but it is probable that he was attempting to reveal some sensitive information, but not to everyone and not immediately.

Boudet was diagnosed with cancer of the intestine in 1914 and the Bishop Beausejour retired him to his home village of Axat, replacing him at Rennes-les-Bains with the Abbé Rescanières. It is widely believed that not long after being given his new posting, Rescanières was visited by two strange visitors and died of poisoning soon after and that the exact same sequence of events happened to Boudet eight weeks later. If this account of events is correct then it would appear that Rescanières had been assassinated by mistake, with the intended victim being Boudet and that the killers had to return a second time to complete the task.

Henri Boudet passed away on 30th March 1915 and was buried in the church yard in Axat in a grave he had personally commissioned to include a prominently raised carving of a closed book displaying the letters IXOIE. This could merely be the Greek word for fish sitting on a copy of the New Testament, but it could have another meaning; for example read in reverse the word becomes 31OXI, or 310 11. The book 'The True Celtic Language and the Cromlech of Rennes-les-Bains', has 310 pages and page eleven speaks of certain keys, which may or may not be the way further into the mystery Boudet has left with us.

The Abbé Antoine Gelis Coustaussa

The third member of the trinity of conspiring priests of the Aude Valley is the Abbé Antoine Gélis of Coustaussa. For many years Gélis met frequently with his friends Saunière and Boudet, but as the 20th century approached he was developing into something of a paranoid recluse, even more than Saunière had become three miles away, over the valley in Rennes-le-Château. Gélis would keep his window shutters locked at all times, even in the height of summer and was extremely cautious about answering his door; only letting in people he knew well.

The calm serenity of the semi-isolated hilltop village of Coustaussa, was shattered on the morning of November 1st 1897 when Ernest Pages, ran into the street dazed and disorientated by the shocking sight he had just witnessed in the presbytery. He had called round to drop off his uncle's mail and surprised to find the door open; he let himself in and found Gélis lying, motionless in a pool of blood.

The priest had been brutally attacked about the head, apparently with a pair of heavy metal fire tongs, but somehow he managed to progress across the room past a table and a window, before he was struck again, this time fatally with an axe. The walls were splattered with blood and Gélis had received 14 head wounds.

The attacker had then laid the body in the position of a priest in repose, with the arms folded on his chest and strangely, with one leg bent up over the other, maybe suggesting a ritual element to the killing. The police found 13,000 francs around the presbytery, enough to live off for 20 years, which would effectively rule out theft. But curiously the attacker had searched the rooms and removed some papers from a briefcase in the bedroom. The assailant had left no evidence to his identity; he had avoided stepping in or touching any blood so left no foot or finger marks, but he must have been well known to Gélis who would not have admitted a stranger into his home.

The police from Couiza carried out the inevitable thorough inquiry, but were faced with a wall of silence from the inhabitants of Caustaussa. Such a violent attack must have involved a significant noise and Gélis must have yelled both in pain and for help, but no one in the village appeared to of heard a sound from the presbytery. The only evidence found at the scene of the crime was, in typical Agatha Christie style, a pack of cigarette papers with the trade-mark 'Tsar' and the enigmatic words 'Viva Angelina', written on one of the papers. Whilst these words led the police nowhere, in 'Rennes-le-Château' (Pg 35), Gérard de Sède suggested they were the passwords to a 'certain ideological group', or secret society. This being the case the positioning of the body must take on a greater significance.

The grave yard in Caustaussa, lies on the outskirts of town, but Anthony Gélis is not to be found within the confines of its whitewashed walls. In the old grave yard, hiding between the buildings in the centre of the village, stands a grave with the word 'Assassine', or 'Murdered' taking central place. This grave is decorated with a fine example of the rose-cross of the Rosicrucians. It is evident that Saunière, Boudet and Gélis shared a secret as well as great wealth, but like his friends Gélis took his covert activities to his grave.

Grave of Antoine Gellis showing the word 'ASSASSINE' – 'Murdered'

Noel Corbu, Henri Buthion and Jean-Luc Robin, the Keepers of the Domain

After the death of Saunière, his trusted housekeeper, confidante and close friend, Marie Dénarnaud, lived a lonely existence in the presbytery for many years between the two World Wars. Then soon after the war ended the Corbu family entered into an annuity agreement with Marie, whereby the family would move into the Villa Bethania and look after her until her death, after which the whole domain would pass to the Noel Corbu. This gave Marie a welcome lease of life until she finally passed away 29th January 1953.

The Corbu family then set about creating a small family run Hotel in the Villa Bethania, and it was Easter Day of 1955 that the Hotel de la Tour started trading with a restaurant and eight guest bed rooms. In its early days, the hotel struggled for clientèle, after all the mystery of Saunière was little known outside the Aude Valley and realising this Corbu set about putting this to rights. He began telling his customers of how the priest, Bérenger Saunière had found treasure in the area and became immensely rich and then as a stroke of luck, the story was picked up by the journalist Albert Salomon. On the three days from 12th January 1956, he published a story in the Depêche du Midi of 'The fabulous discovery of the millionaire priest of Rennes-le-Château. With just one swing of his pick at the altar pillar, the Abbé Saunière uncovers the treasure of Blanche of Castille'.

The rooms at the Hotel de la Tour now filled up as tourists and gold diggers flocked to Rennes, thanks to Salomon's welcome publicity, but Corbu was thinking of new ventures. He sold the domain to a frequent visitor and gold digger, Jean Pellet, from Lyon and his business partner and occultist, Henri Buthion. Soon after the curse of Rennes-le-Château caught up with Noel Corbu and he was involved in a tragic and fatal accident. Whilst driving between Castelnaudary and Carcassonne in the middle of the night, he collided with a stationary lorry and his Renault 16 did not have a chance.

One of the new owners of the Rennes-le-Château domain, Henri Buthion also had a brush with the grim reaper, when in 1973 he came under a fire arms attack and his car was riddled with bullets. He survived the incident but was reluctant to speak of it; however it was starting to appear dangerous to get to close to the secrets of Rennes-le-Château.

It was in 1994 that Jean-Luc Robin took over the running of the Saunière domain. Henri Buthion had recently sold the business on to foreign investors and Jean-Luc had taken the position of manager, with the intension of setting up a museum and eventually the La Table de l'Abbé restaurant in the gardens. Robin had spent many happy childhood years in the Languedoc and was happy to return to this beautiful area and having been a previously successful restaurateur, he set about developing and running the domain.

Over the years Jean-Luc added greatly to the sum of knowledge surrounding the Saunière mystery and had been responsible for writing two fascinating books on the subject. After fourteen years living in Rennes-le-Château, Robin successfully stood for election as deputy mayor of the village and was about to use his new position of power to confront the mayor with his ideas of how to preserve the domain and commence some selective excavations. Unfortunately Jean-Luc Robin suffered a sudden and unexpected heart attack in March 2008 just three days after being voted in as deputy mayor.

Chapter 6

The Mystery of the Two Towers

The most striking feature of the domaine that Saunière constructed at Rennes-le-Château is the Tour Magdala, standing at the corner of the garden with the most wonderful view over the valley. The priest could have stood on top of his tour and viewed not only his home town of Montazels but a 360 degree panorama of the entire valley.

The tower was a copy of one that used to stand in the Spanish town of Girona where Saunière often visited from 1888. Patrice Chaplin, who used to be married to Charlie Chaplin's son and who had many years of association with Girona, researched the 'House of Canons', where the tower was constructed in 1851. She records her stunning, discoveries about Saunière's visits and the strange occult group which would meet at the house to carry out magic rituals associated with the Holy Grail, in her book 'City of Secrets'.

Chaplin uncovered many letters which provided proof of the activities in Girona, including one telling example, written on 6th February 1901 by Saunière to Maria Tourdes saying;

'I will arrive Wednesday late so please wait up for me. Otherwise leave the other door open. I will bring some plants. Can you find out the measurements of the foundations [of the tower] and if they know how that precise figure was arrived at? You will have to go and see

The Cathar Country

the architect, or better still, ask Dalmas to go. He must get a copy of the plans.' (Chaplin, Patrice, *City of Secrets*).

*The Tour Magdala (Rennes 1906) and
The Torre Magdala (Girona 1851)*

Maria Tourdes was a French woman from Quillan who appears to have been put into position by Saunière and his friend, Ernest Cros, the archaeologist who first recorded the carvings on the head-stone of Mary de Blanchfort. Known locally as the 'French Woman', Tourdes appears to have lived a semi-isolated life, keeping the house for and receiving large sums of money from both Bérenger and Alfred Saunière.

Spanish locals, who knew Saunière, told Chaplin that the priest first visited the town following coded instructions left by the Abbé Bigou, who had found his way there after fleeing across the border in 1792. It appears that the tower at Girona was of great importance to the trail left by Bigou, so Saunière provided the finance required to purchase the property.

The occult group in Girona is said to have been involved in rituals and ceremonial magic connected with the Grail. Chaplin reported from her interviews with her source that

Saunière had discovered a 'secret' and spoke of the Grail using references from 'Wolfram von Eschenbach's, Parzival'.

'He described it as being made of the most remarkable physical matter in the universe. It was purported to give powers beyond human reach including physical longevity, immortality, and invisibility. Who holds this, holds the world. It has power of projection and takes the bearer out of time. It produces levitation. Objects move out of the dimensions as we know them and reappear elsewhere. They've not disappeared. They've just travelled beyond our sight and come back. He mentioned transmutation, teleportation. It's a gift from paradise, known since the beginning of time.' (Chaplin Patrice, *City of Secrets*).

The group practiced certain rituals, which Bigou also used to carry out. The process would involve fasting, purification rites and lengthy meditation. They would aim for a heightened state of awareness through the incantation of sacred texts for days on end. Then having reached a state of pure consciousness they would call up the highest level entity, the 'bearer of the cup'. The ceremony was said to use the Grail to open up a 'portal', linking north and south, using twin towers. They were interested in utilising the energy produced by magically connecting two towers and this could have been the reason that the second identical tower was constructed at Rennes-les-Château. This concept of bringing together two opposites is fundamental in the mystery training of the Cabbala and on the 'Tree of Life', this is represented by the two pillars of 'mercy and severity', with the coming together of these two poles at the pillar of 'Equilibrium'. This connection to Gnostic Dualistic thought is reminiscent of the belief system of the Cathars and it is thought that Saunière would give a form consolamentum to the dying in the same way that the Cathar Perfects would have done.

Also at Rennes-les-Château there is a further identical tower connected to the Tour Magdala by a raised curved walk-way. If Saunière was carrying out the twin tower rituals at Rennes, then the participants would have regarded this walkway as a place of great power and it was here that he sat in an armchair after he passed away. He was visited in this position of repose by unknown guests who each passed by him and took a tassel from his coat. This strange ceremony has never been explained, but if the tales are true and a portal had been opened between the two towers, then Saunière had been placed directly on its probable location.

The Orangery Tower at Rennes

The second tower at Rennes-le-Château is an Orangery with a glass upper section and it is difficult not to draw some link with the events of September 11th 2001, which also involved twin towers of glass and produced a huge amount of energy.

Another Two Towers have been very much in the public eye since the release of the film of that name in 2002, which was taken from JRR. Tolkien's trilogy 'Lord of the Rings'. This best selling master-piece was written between 1937 and 1949 and included many hidden magical references. In an early scene in the first book, 'The Fellowship of the Ring', the wizard Gandalf threw a ring into the fire at Bag End, the home of the hobbit, Bilbo Baggins. A similar story from Girona involves a ring which Saunière cast into a fire during a ceremony and which was cherished as a charm of protection by Maria Tourdes. In the film the ring had an inscription written in Tolkien's language 'Black Speech' and Saunière's had the inscription BS. Maybe this is just one of those strange coincidences, but the same two letters can be found above the statue of Asmodius, which Saunière had placed just inside the church of St Mary Magdalene.

Saunière's magical workings were referred to in a letter again uncovered by Patrice Chaplin;

'The French priest must have trusted her not only in terms of investment but also on a scientific level. I saw a note he left her on the energy produced between two towers. She was there when the ring was thrown into the fire. She has seen so much... he frightened her to death.' Also on May 13th 1897; *'I know Sion', Bérenger did talk about North and South, explaining how they must be unified.'* (Chaplin Patrice, *City of Secrets*).

The Cathar Country

Was this a reference to the Priory of Sion, the secret society that appears periodically during the story of Rennes-le Château?

It is possible that Saunière may have had doubts about his new found practices and was quoted as saying to one Juli Tarres, in Girona, that;

'he was in it too deeply to get out. He spoke of a ritual, -the ceremony-, uniting 'North and South.' 'It transcends time and space as we know it.' 'A portal. A work he had to accomplish. Perhaps the greatest magical working any magician could aim towards'. He was also quoted as saying that 'he knew that if he gave up any information, they would kill him'. (Chaplin Patrice, *City of Secrets*).

On a letter written on paper from the Hotel Eden au Lac in Montreux, Saunière wrote words reminiscent of the letter Nicolas Fouquet received from his brother Louis Fouquet after his meeting with Nicolas Poussin, which read;

'Since the death of my grandmother, I have decided that the wisest solution is to transfer the materials to FD. I understand that this is perhaps not what she would have wanted, but in today's world that can hardly enter my considerations. GT has assured me that the Vatican was always aware of its existence. 'The friends' here as well as in Girona have advanced the theory that it involves one of the biggest secrets of our time, of all times and I am intent on burying it. Upon my word, let someone else find it. Furthermore, they're challenging my rights. Consequently, could you see that the attached instructions and documents are transmitted to the person named above. Your friend, CCC and Marie Corvese.

P.S. The scandal that could break wouldn't be good for anyone.' (Chaplin Patrice, *City of Secrets*).

As with everything that Saunière constructed or adapted at Rennes-les-Château, both towers have magical symbolism built into their fabric. For example there is a connection to the Cabbalistic Tree of life in that they each have 22 steps, corresponding to the 22 paths between the sephiroth. These paths are of immense importance to practitioners of the magical arts and represent the same 22 aspects of consciousness as do the Major Arcana of the original Tarot and consequently, the 22 letters of the Hebrew alphabet.

The addition of all this added symbolism resulted in a massive cost of 45,000 francs for the Tour Magdala, which should really have been quite a simple construction. This would have taken one local worker 41 years to build at the average wage of the time, which was a meagre 3 francs per day. The interior of the tower was converted into an elegant and comfortable wooden library, where Saunière had a collection of over 1,000 religious and occult books. He also had a strong metal defensive door fitted at the entrance to the turret, which would be crucial if any intruder was spotted approaching from the panoramic view from the top of the tower.

The magical connection between the Tour Magdela in France and the Torre Magdala in Spain came to an end in 1962, when the local authority in Girona purchased the House of Canons and demolished its tower. Today you can still visit the garden and sit on the steps which used to lead up to the tower but any workings, which may have taken place, are now terminated permanently.

The British Tower

Standing on the outskirts of Glastonbury, at the side of the busy A39 in Somerset, England, there is a large eccentric building which goes by the name of 'Chilton Priory', although it has never been an ecclesiastical building. On the corner of the building is a tower, which looks strangely similar to the ones at Rennes-les-Château and Girona.

The Tower at Chilton Priory (1838)

Glastonbury is believed by many to be the spiritual centre of Britain and like Rennes-les-Château and Girona the area is immersed in the myths of the Holy Grail. The Knight Templars, whose homeland could be said to have been in the Languedoc, also owned a huge amount of land around Glastonbury. This included the whole of ancient Bristol and also the nearby village of Templecombe, where you can still find a painting of a head, once the property of the Templars.

Chilton Priory was constructed by the high grade freemason, William Stradling, beginning with the tower and a rear wing in 1838. Starting life as a folly, the property eventually became a large country house containing an eclectic collection of artefacts. It is not known how far Stradling's Masonic activities went, but he was known to be in the upper grades of his order and so would have been involved in advanced rituals. He had many of the floors of the priory laid out in the black and white checker design used in Masonic ceremonies and as we see below, he could have been a member of an order connected with grail magic, much as Saunière had been.

Katharine Maltwood
(1878-1961)

In 1917 (the year of Saunière's death), Katharine Emma Maltwood purchased Chilton Priory with her husband John. They lived in the house for over 20 years and it was during this time, Katharine discovered the Glastonbury Zodiac, in 1925, as a result of her in-depth research into the myths and legends of the Holy Grail and the Arthurian romances, which she considered to be present in the landscapes surrounding Glastonbury and her home. Part of her theory was that the Glastonbury Zodiac represented a grail-related ritual landscape, types of which could be found around the world at points of particular spiritual importance. These hot-spots were associated with ancient mystery cults, which may have been the holders of a body of wisdom, which has been passed down through the ages to some of the occult societies of today.

The Cathar Country

A large part of Katherine's early studies in the 1890's took place in Paris, where she was involved with the same secret societies that Saunière had been introduced to during his visits there beginning in 1891. A prominent name of note being Joséphin Peladan and his 'Ordre de la Rose et Croix Catholique de Temple et du Graal'.

Katharine worked in her study, which like Sauniere's, was located in the tower. Her work on the Glastonbury Zodiac and the grail led her further into the realms of occultism and freemasonry, which she saw as a way to connect with the secrets of the 'Temple of the Stars' and the zodiacs. In 1931 Katharine joined the female order, the 'Ancient Masonry, Grand Lodge of England' and also planed a new order called 'The Honourable Fraternity of Ancient Masonry'.

From her researches Katharine believed that the author of 'Perlesvaus' or the 'High History of the Holy Grail', which was a continuation of Chrétien de Troyes unfinished Percival, was in fact a Knights Templar. Considering that both the Templars and the early Grail Romances, both came out of the Courts of the Count of Champaign around the same time, this would not appear to be an unworthy hypothesis. She saw the Templars as the traditional guardians of the Holy Grail and made a connection with a British Masonic order, which used ancient nature initiation rights of Egypt and Greece. Katharine believed that William Stradling was a member of this order and it was for this reason that he built Chilton Priory, beginning with the tower, on the spot he did, which she discovered during her researches to be an old pilgrimage route to Glastonbury.

Chapter 7

The Emerald Temple of Rennes

There is no denying the beauty of the landscapes surrounding Rennes-le-Château. The awe-inspiring mountainsides covered in Beech, Silver Fir and vineyards, have an unusually relaxing effect on visitors that belies the tragic cruelty which has taken place here in the name of God. It is nearly impossible to imagine how such stark inhumanity could have occurred in such a place. But is there, as has been suggested in numerous books, more to the peace and tranquillity of this area of the Languedoc? Are we looking at a sacred landscape, laid out in antiquity to emphasise the power of these lands and to create a protected holy sanctuary for its inhabitants and their secrets?

The Temple of Venus, Isis and the Magdalene

Writer and researcher Henry Lincoln made the remarkable discovery of a geometrically perfect pentagram with mountain peaks marking each point and with a sixth mountain lying at its centre. Lincoln's research into the geometry of the area began with the study of Poussin's Shepherds of Arcadia painting. After receiving instructions in a letter from Gerard de Sede, Lincoln located the tomb shown in the Shepherds painting on the D613 from Couiza to Arques, the same road that Jesus looks down in the church of Mary Magdelene (see chapter 4) and he noticed the similarity between the surrounding mountains and the background in the painting.

The Cathar Country

This discovery led to an analysis of the painting by Professor Christopher Cornford, of the Royal Collage of Art, an expert in the geometrical composition of art works. Cornford found that the Shepherds of Arcadia was based on a pentagonal structure and suggested that it would be helpful to examine a map of the area for a similar structure.

Lincoln began with the mountain peaks that held significant ancient structures; Rennes-le-Château, the Templar Château of Bezu and the Château of Blanchefort and established that they sat in perfect association with each other and that they formed a pentagonal triangle. The next step was obviously to locate the remaining two points of the pentagram and amazingly these were also located on the mountain summits of, La Soulane and Serre de Lauzet and as if by way of a bonus the slopes of the mountain of La Pique lie at the centre of the whole design.

We now have a perfectly formed pentagram, in the landscape formed out of mountain peaks, a natural temple, invisible, yet very much present in the landscape around Rennes-le-Château. The pentagram has a definite association with Venus, as this is the only planet that forms an exact geometric shape in the skies, on its travels through the skies, as viewed from Earth. On its eight year orbital cycle Venus creates a geometrically accurate pentagram.

The Cathar Country

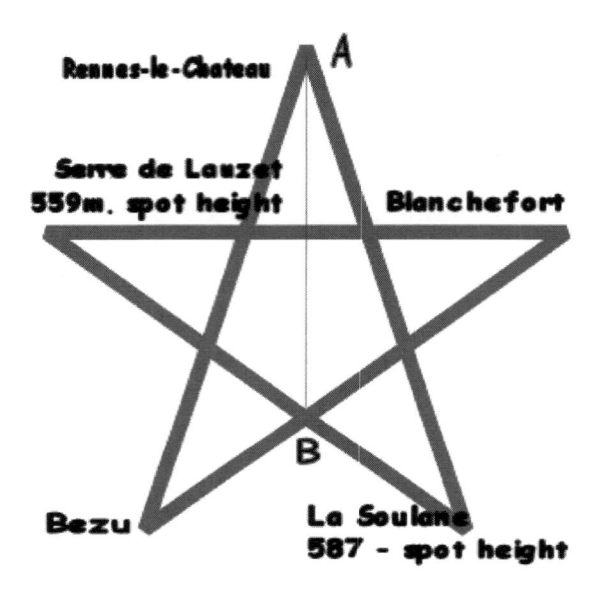

```
         A
Rennes-le-Chateau

Serre de Lauzet
559m. spot height      Blanchefort


                B
Bezu           La Soulane
               587 - spot height
```

*Lincoln's Pentagram of Mountains.
Also showing the length AB, which forms the hexagram and
the distance between many churches.*

The knights Templar would have been aware of this and the age old mystical teaching of the Emerald Tablet, written down and recorded as part of the voluminous esoteric works, under the name of Hermes Trismegistus (Hermes the three times great);

'True, without falsehood, certain and most true, that which is above is as that which is below, and that which is below is as that which is above, for the performance of the miracles of the One Thing. And as all things are from One, by the mediation of One, so all things have their birth from this One Thing by adaptation. The Sun is its father, the Moon its mother, and the Wind carries it in its belly, its nurse is

the Earth. This is the father of all perfection, or consummation of the whole world. Its power is integrating, if it be turned into earth.

Thou shalt separate the earth from the fire, the subtle from the gross, suavely, and with great ingenuity. It ascends from earth to heaven and descends again to earth, and receives the power of the superiors and of the inferiors. So thou hast the glory of the whole world; therefore let all obscurity flee before thee. This is the strong force of all forces, overcoming every subtle and penetrating every solid thing. So the world was created. Hence were all wonderful adaptations, of which this is the manner. Therefore am I called Hermes Trismegistus, having the three parts of the philosophy of the whole world. What I have to tell is completed, concerning the Operation of the Sun.' (Trismegistus, Hermes, *Emerald Tablet*).

This wonderful passage is the source of the much quoted phrase, 'As above, so below' and in the case of our Temple of Rennes, this saying comes alive in a very real and tangible sense, with the pentagram of Venus forming the cathedral roof for the pentagram of mountains.

In the western esoteric mystery tradition Venus is equivalent to the goddesses of Aphrodite, Hathor and Isis, which became equivalent to the Magdalene. The church at Rennes-le-Château, which is dedicated to Mary Magdalene, is built on the foundations of an earlier temple of Isis; thus showing a connection between the church and the landscape Temple. There are many organisations today that hold this so called 'Black Maddonna' of Isis and the Magdalene, to be sacred.

Taking the geometry one step further, lines can be drawn across the points of the first pentagram, to form a larger one sharing the same centre. The northwest point of the new pentagram rests incredibly on the cave of the Magdalene, found on the side of the road near the town of Arques and still used by members of the various Isis/Madonna sects for meetings and ceremonies. There is a local legend that Mary Magdalene lived in a cave in this area having fled Jerusalem after the crucifixion, with the son from her marriage with Jesus.

Three of the other points of the larger pentagram also lie on significant locations; the south-eastern section points at the mountain of Bugarach, which has a supernatural tradition that inspired Jules Verne to write about an underground world, with strange plants and inhabited by stranger creatures. The northern point rests on the small medieval town of Alet-les-Bains, which has a fine history of philosophy and boasts a house associated with Nostradamus, the remains of fine old abbey, an 'Old Bishop's Palace', healing spa waters and a small Cathar type church on a mountain high above the town. The north-eastern point lies on the edge of a second geometric shape hiding in the countryside; a hexagram of churches.

A hexagram of churches

The hexagram was located by using the measurement from the centre of the pentagram to the intersection of the cords (AB), (see pg. 168), which Lincoln noticed to be a unit of length often repeated on the map, joining many items together, for example;

Rennes-les-Bains Church	to	*Le Bezu Church*
Rennes-les-Bains Church	to	*Rennes-le-Chateau Castle*
Rennes-les-Bains Church	to	*The Aven*
Rennes-les-Bains Church	to	*Bezu Ruin*

Laval Church	to	*St Just Church*
Auriac Church	to	*St.Pancrasse Church*
Sougraigne Church	to	*La Pique*
Les Sauzils Church	to	*Ginoles Church*
Les Sauzils Church	to	*St Ferriol Church*
Croux Church	to	*Bouriege Church*
Campagne-sur-Aude Church	to	*The Aven*
St Julia Church	to	*The Aven*
Luc Church	to	*Serres Church*
Veraza Church	to	*Poussin Tomb*
La Soulane	to	*Poussin Tomb*
Castillou Church	to	*Poussin Tomb*
Campagne-sur-Aude Church	to	*Rennes-le-Chateau*
Calvaire NW of Autugnac	to	*Rennes-le-Chateau*

(Lincoln, Henry, *The Holy Place*, pg120)

The church at Esperaza is connected to an extraordinary number of other churches by the same measure. Using this church as a centre and the unit AB as diameter, the resulting circle passes through the churches of Coustaussa, Granes, St Ferriol and Les Sauzils and the latter two were also separated by the same AB measure. It is possible therefore to project this measure from St Ferriol to Les Sauzils around the circumference and using the points of intersection with the circle to draw in a hexagram. The completion of this second geometrical figure adds the churches of Montazels, Fa, Antugnac and a roadside Calvaire, or cross bringing to nine the number of significant holy sites covered.

In a similar way that the pentagram has been used traditionally as an occult symbol, the hexagram has an analogous pedigree. The hexagram has been described as;

'A geometric figure which has six points, formed from two interlinking triangles: The two triangles correspond to opposing forces of fire and water. The hexagram shows these rival energies balanced and in harmony with each other. Also called the "Star of David" and the "Star of the Macrocosm". It is also a symbol of the perfected human being, and signifies the Hermetic principal of "As above, so below". The penetration of one triangle by another is also said to represent the penetration of man's lower nature by the higher and divine forces.' (Regardie, Israel, *The Tree of Life*, pg457).

Wood's Genisis

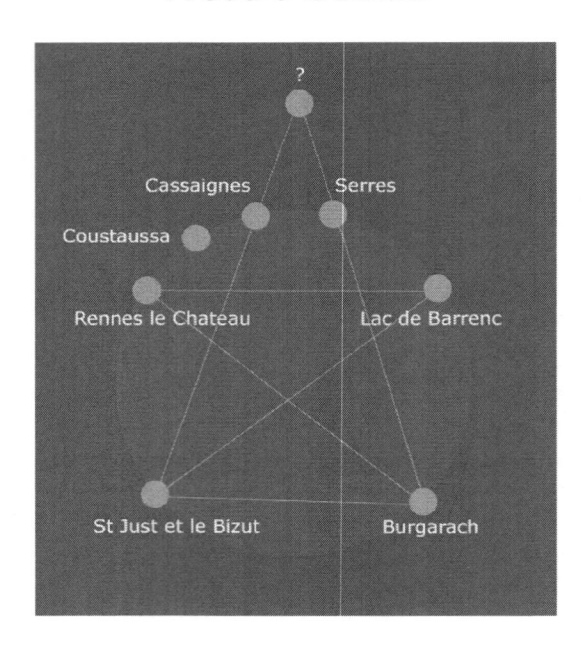

David Wood's Landscape Pentagram

The Cathar Country

David Wood combined his skills in trigonometrical and aerial surveying, with a keen enthusiasm in the mysteries of Rennes-le-Château and spent many years researching the landscapes of the surrounding valley, studying the maps of the area and the relationships between significant land-marks. With the help of advances in computerised mapping technology, which would enable him to accurately measure distances and angles with an accuracy of within a few feet, Wood produced some fascinating results in his first book 'Genisis', in 1985.

The structure Wood had discovered covered an area of some 40 square miles and had, in his opinion, originally been marked out by standing stones and other megalithic sites. Through the passage of time, these places had remained important and had become the positions for future constructions such as churches, way-side crosses, castles and towns. But most remarkable is Wood's insistence that the early Druidic people, who would have laid out the original ground plan, must have had advanced surveying skills, the likes of which we have only recently been able to match with the use of GPS, (Global Positioning Systems). Wood also makes an association between his discoveries and ancient Egypt, suggesting that it could have been the people of the first Egyptian Dynasty (2920-2770 BC), who had instructed the positioning of this landscape monument, to provide a message in the language of mathematics, for future civilisations. A message that was hidden, only to be uncovered at a time when mankind would again have the sophisticated technologies to read it, in the last part of an Earthly cycle, the time which came before a catastrophe or deluge.

Although the original mountain pentagram had triggered wood's interest in the geometry of the area, he did not use this as his starting point and instead began with the sunrise line from Rennes-le-Château church to Blanchefort, which takes place on the saint's day of St Mary Magdalene on 22nd July. This line continues through Blanchefort to the church at Arques and taking a right angle at Blanchefort leads to the church at Rennes-les-Bains. The line from Rennes-le-Château to Arques is six English miles long and even more astoundingly; this is crossed by the old French meridian line, or Rose Line, at exactly four miles, or two thirds of its length.

In his enigmatic book 'The True Celtic Language and The Stone Circles of Rennes-les-Bains', the priest Henri Boudet wrote of English as the original World language, but whilst he gave many strange examples, he seemed to have omitted an explanation as to where the stone circles fitted into the picture. The use of the generic term 'stone circles', appears to refer more properly to any megalithic structure and in fact, Boudet's title used the word Chromlech, which is a form of chambered tomb. After publication Boudet's book received pretty much exclusively negative feedback, but this was mixed with confusion as the author was well known as an academic, with a sound foundation and reputation for producing highly intellectual work. How could such a person suddenly produce this work of apparent nonsense? Looking at Boudet's work in the light of David Wood's findings, may produce some clarity. Was the English language, in fact the language of mathematics, with the English mile as its unit length? Was this language spoken silently in the landscape around Boudet's parish and punctuated in megalithic structures, marking out vital and pivotal positions.

Continuing the process of geometry, Wood located the centre point for his new pentagram, by drawing in the line from the

The Cathar Country

Poussin Tomb to Rennes-les-Bains, which passed through his original line from Rennes-le-Château to Arques exactly at the point of the meridian. He then extended this line by one mile passed Rennes-les-Bains and used the end as his centre point. He found that a circle with a diameter of six miles, scribed from this point went through Rennes-le-Château, Bugarach, St Just-et-el-Bezu, Coustaussa and the Château of Serre. He was then able to use the positions of St Just and Bugarach as the two lower points of his pentagram, with Rennes-le-Château as the North West point and the position of Serres to draw in the remainder of his landscape temple. (See pg. 172)

Since Henry Lincoln first published his geometrical findings in the BBC2 Chronicle programme, 'The Lost Treasure of Jerusalem?' in March 1971, the body of work on the subject has been added to by many and varied contributors, with results and conclusions ranging from slightly unusual to the extremely impressive. What ever the outcome of this ongoing and for ever intriguing aspect of the Cathar Country, it is clear that the area is special and that a sacred ambience can be detected in the air.

Chapter 8

The Knights Templar
The true Knights of the Grail

The majority of the wealthy and leading families of the Languedoc in the early 12th centaury, through the Albigensian crusade and into the 14th centaury, had strong Cathar and Knights Templar allegiances. The area was known as a Templar stronghold and the Blanchfort dynasty of Rennes-le-Château provided a grand-master of the order. But who were these infamous warrior monks that most people have heard of but know little about, why were they formed and what was their goal?

Formation of the Templars
The orthodox account

The formation of the Knights Templar is shrouded in mystery, mistaken information and possibly deliberate misinformation. As in so many historical subject areas early accounts comfortably fill the void of knowledge and are adopted by academia as the true story. Books are written, careers built and reputations formed around the official account of events, which must now be preserved and unquestioned. This has the unfortunate effect of stifling the growth of the subject and understanding of the real circumstances, which later study brings to the fore. Moreover if early accounts of a story are taken directly from a source, which may have a secret to protect, the official version of events may cover a much more intriguing story.

In the case of the Knights Templar it was Guillaume de Tyre, a Frankish historian and Archbishop of Tyre, a small town in Lebanon, who provided the first accounts between 1175 and 1185, over fifty years after the formation of the order. It is not clear where he sourced his information about these events, which occurred well before his life-time, but it is probable that he was reporting a history that the Templars themselves were promoting. Although these accounts of the early days of the Templars have been adopted by most future historians as fact, it is prudent to use de Tyre's work only as a framework and a foundation to build a more complete story.

The Cathar Country

In de Tyre's orthodox narrative, the Templars were formed by Hugues de Payen, a vassal of the Count of Champagne, in 1118 to protect pilgrims travelling to the holy land. The newly formed order travelled to Jerusalem, or 'Outremer', the 'lands beyond the sea', as they were known to the Templars. Here they were granted an audience with King Baldwin I, in what became the last year of his reign. Part of the Jerusalem royal palace was built on the foundations of Solomon's Temple and it was this lavish wing that the king made available to the order as accommodation and headquarters; thus providing them with the name 'The Poor Knights of Christ and the Temple of Solomon', which eventually became reduced to the 'Knights Templar'.

Guillaume de Tyres tells of how the Templars kept their numbers to nine for the first nine years of their existence and that they spent this time patrolling the highways and trails of Outremer. As well as direct information from the Templars of the time, de Tyre's work would also have been based on the chronicles of Fulcher of Chartres, who was born in Chartres around 1059 and as such was contemporary with the formation of the Templars. After the conquest of Jerusalem in 1099, Fulcher had travelled there on pilgrimage, with Baldwin of Boulogne the future king and had acted as Chaplin and chronicler.

Fulcher's extensive work was divided into three books covering consecutive time periods; firstly the preparation for the first crusade in 1095, the conquest of Jerusalem and the establishment of Godfrey of Bouillon as the first ruler; secondly Baldwin I, the second king from 1100 to 1118 and

The Cathar Country

thirdly Baldwin II up to 1127 when Fulcher probably died in a plague which took over Jerusalem. Throughout his writings, which took place between 1109 until his death, not one mention was made of the Knight Templar, which would go some way to disprove the theory that they were highly active in the area. It would be a lot more logical to suggest that the nine Templars were acting on an isolated or even secret project.

The leading knights returned to France in 1128, where on the 14th January Bernard of Clairvaux used the 'Council of Troyes', held at the home of Theobald II, Count of Champagne, to put the Knights Templar on a more firm footing.

Bernard of Clairvaux
(1090 – August 20, 1153)

Bernard de Fontaine was born into the nobility of Burgandy, as one of the sons of the Lord of Fontaines and Aleth of Montband. At the age of nineteen his mother died and Bernard decided on a life of devotion as a Cistercian monk.

At this time the Cistercian Order had only been in operation for eleven years, having been founded by Robert of Molesme in 1098, with the opening of Cîteaux Abbey near Dijon, around 100 miles south of Troyes. When Bernard joined the order in 1112, he was followed by around thirty of his relatives and friends, nearly doubling its membership. In 1115 Bernard travelled to the Val d'Absinthe, 40 miles southeast of Troyes, with a band of twelve fellow monks, where he founded a monastery on the 25th June of that year. Bernard named the area Claire Valley, but this soon developed into the Clairvaux

179

(Valley of Light) and it is from this base that the new Abbot of Clairvaux became highly influential in a massive expansion of the Cistercian Order.

It is helpful to view the meteoric rise of St. Bernard within the Cistercian order and its association with the Knights Templar, in the context of his family connections and his position, both geographically and in society. The land on which the monastery of Clairvaux was built had been donated by the count of Champagne, whose extensive territories east of Paris, were larger than the country of Wales. Hugues de Payen, the first Templar grand master, was a vassal of the count as were at least two of his companions, who were also neighbours and relatives and one of the original knights, Andre de Montbard was Bernard's uncle. It was under Bernard's influence that the Templar order was officially accepted by the pope, at the Council of Troyes, under the rule of St. Benedict, which Bernard had already altered to meet the needs of the Cistercian order.

Bernard of Clairvaux also had both personal and philosophical links with the mystery schools and the initiatory custom. Many of the leaders of the school at Chartres Cathedral including; Bernard of Chartres, John of Salisbury and Alanus ab Insulis were members of the Cistercian order.

Hugh I, the Count of Champagne
(1074–1125 – Count from 1093)

In his time, Hugh of Champagne was one of the most powerful French noblemen; his godfather was non other than King Philippe I of France. His family was linked to many of the power-houses of Europe including; the French and Scottish St. Clairs, the Dukes of Burgundy and Normandy, and the Plantagenet kings of England. The capital of Hugh's Champagne region was the city of Troyes, which became a centre of esoteric philosophy and cabbalistic teaching and attracted a large Jewish population. Probably the most prominent cabalistic scholar, arising from the Jewish community of Troyes, became a friend of Hugh of Campagne and often visited his court. This was the Rabbi Solomon be Isaac, who came to fame under the name 'Rachi'. Great similarities can be made between the county of Champagne and the lands of the leading families of the Languedoc, where esoteric and cabalistic teachings also had the freedom to take hold and grow.

As a side issue it is of interest that the original sparkling wine, which became famous under the Champagne appellation, was originally produced in the Languedoc.

In 1104 Hugh of Champagne spent around four years in the Holy Land and set out for Jerusalem again in 1114. This time he had the intention of joining the Templars, who were then known as 'la Milice du Christ', or the 'Militia of Christ'. Huge put off his initiation until 1124 and after his second visit to the Holy Land, quickly returned home to Troyes and immediately donated the lands to the Cistercians where Bernard of Clairvaux built his abbey.

The Council of Troyes

In 1128, four years after Hugh I, Count of Champagne joined the Knight Templar, the papal legate Cardinal Matthew

The Cathar Country

d'Albano, called a clerical summit meeting in Troyes, which was attended by leading European churchmen and various French nobleman. The Council of Troyes opened on 14th January and from the beginning it was clear that it was going to be the Bernard of Clairvaux show and that he had a one point agenda, to legitimise the Templar order by bringing it into the body of the church.

The council was being held at the court of the Count of Champagne, one of the most powerful men in Europe, with blood ties to the king of Jerusalem and the Templars and the Pope just could not afford to get into conflict with him. This gave Bernard, who had been working hard on adapting the rule of St. Benedict to fit both the Cistercian and the Templar orders, a free hand to unravel his plans. Two weeks into the council, on the 31st January 1128, Hugues de Payen, the Grand Master of the Knight Templar, together with his colleagues received their new Holy Rule', as prepared by Bernard of Clairvaux. They were then an official order of the Church of Rome.

Pope Honorius II may well have found the opportunity of gaining a powerful and growing religious militia under his own control, quite appealing. It would be much better to be running such a body than have it existing in the Holy Land and Europe, with the possibility of it becoming an enemy of the church, some time in the future.

This mastery of political proceedings by Bernard of Clairvaux showed its hand again, when after the death of Honorius II in 1130, Bernard managed to manoeuvre the highly controversial, Gregorio Paperechi into the papacy, under the name of Innocent II (Pope from 1130 – 1143). Under this Pope and his successor, Celestine II (Guido di Castello, ope from 1143 to 1144), the power of the Templars increased massively as a result of three papal Bulls. In 1139 Innocent II issued the 'Omne datum optimun', a papal bull making the Templars answerable only to the Pope, thus giving them a relative free hand to do and act in whatever way they liked, without the inconvenience of having to pay taxes or tithes.

The Rex Deus Families

The work and researches of Marilyn Hopkins, Graham Simmans and Tim-Wallace Murphy has uncovered a family lineage called the Rex Deus, which they claim to be direct descendants from the select high priests of the Temple of Jerusalem, which includes the immediate descendants of Jesus. These families who are the keepers of much sacred knowledge spread out around the world and went underground for the sake of safety. During the Dark Ages the families blended into the cultures, in which they found themselves, outwardly taking on the prominent religion of the area, in order to avoid the vicious heresy laws of the catholic church of Rome.

In the days of the Herodian Temple of Jerusalem, the High Priests would teach at two boarding schools for the families of the line of Levi, one for boys and one for girls. Of these families it was the line of Cohen, which was bound by Jewish law to marry within the family and to become High Priests. The male pupils were destined to high office and the Cohens were to take their place as High priests in their turn. The High Priest tutors were responsible for the impregnation of the female pupils in order to keep the bloodline pure. These young girls would then be found a husband within the Jewish nobility and the resulting child would be returned to the temple school at the age of seven to be educated.

A record of the fate of one the female pupils of the High Priest school, gives a fascinating indication of how biblical accounts of real events can be misunderstood and how legends are created. The girl in question was called Miriam and in history she is known as Mary. When Mary came of age she was impregnated by a High Priest by the name of Gabriel, which was one of the names that the High Priests would take, that included the names of angels and other characters from Jewish history. Now that she was pregnant, she rejected the first husband that had been found for her, so a replacement was sought by lot from among the appropriate families. The suitor was a young man of the Davidic line by the name of Joseph of Tyre, an ancestor of Hyram, the King of Tyre, who is prominent in Masonic legend as Hiram Abif. The husband of Mary is known to us today as St. Joseph and the child from the union with the High Priest was Jesus, who after spending his first few years in Egypt, was returned to the Temple school at the appropriate time to be educated.

Over the many years that the Rex Deus families have remained out of sight, they have been establishing themselves within the leading families of the societies they have adopted. Throughout the history of the Knights Templar, the Languedoc and the Holy Land, we find the names of the Rex Deus families. Amongst these are; the Scottish Sinclair's, Lords of Rosslyn and the Leslie clan, the Saxon dynasty, the Counts of Champagne, Godfroi de Bouillon, the first patriarch of Jerusalem and the Habsburgs of the Austro-Hungarian Empire and many more illustrious names from history.

The Habsburg, Maximilian I (1459 – 1519), the son of Frederick III, the Holy Roman Emperor and Eleanor of Portugal, was King of the Romans from 1493 and Holy Roman Emperor from 1508 until his death. He designed his own musoleum which clearly displayed his Rex Deus connection, through 40 life-size statues of his ancestors.   Amongst these were depictions of; the Merovingian King Clovis, Godfroi de Bouillon, Queen Elizabeth of Hungary, King Ferdinand of Aragon, Philip Duke of Burgundy, Archduke Sigismund and the Duchess Mary of Burgundy.

The existence of a recurring family bloodline, albeit largely unrecognised, would indicate an unseen force operating in the background of world events throughout history. These powerful cabals of interlocked families with their own goals may have been working behind the scenes towards their universal aims. If nothing else the recognition that events may be connected by these active bloodlines, could help in explaining some of the extraordinary happenings and riddles of past events.

The Temple Mount Timeline

To put the activities of the Knight Templar, the Rex Deus families and events in the Languedoc into further context, it is helpful to take a look at the timeline of the temples built on the Temple Mount in Jerusalem.

Solomon succeeded David as king of Israel and the first temple to be constructed was Solomon's Temple ('Beit HaMikdash' – 'The House of That Which is Holy'). It was completed in 960BC on Moriah Hill, to act as a centre for the religion of the Israelites and a place to house the Ark of the Covenant, together with others holy relics. This temple was eventually destroyed by the Babylonian king Nebuchadnezzar in 586BC;

'Nebuchadnezzar attacked Jerusalem again and under the leadership of his captain of the guard who burned the Temple in 586/587 BCE along with the king's house, and all the houses of Jerusalem, and every great man's house. The city wall was broken down, and the rest of the people that were left in the city, and the fugitives that fell away to the king of Babylon, with the remnant of the multitude, were carried away'. (2 Kings 25).

Work on the Second Temple ('Beit HaMikdash – 'The Temple House') began in 535BC and was completed in 516BC, during the time of the Persian Empire. It stood until 4th August 70AD, when it was destroyed by Titus during the Roman Siege of Jerusalem, which ended the Jewish revolt of 66AD.

The second temple was later known as Herod's Temple as it was King Herod the Great, who had carried out a massive expansion on the temple mount and the temple buldings, which involved extensive rebuilding of the original structure, around 19BC.

The Roman invaders built palaces and a Temple of Jupiter on the site of the ruined temple, together with various other constructions. Much later around 690, the Dome of the Rock was built and most of the earlier temple remains removed. Today you can still see a step leading to the Dome of the Rock, which was the capstone of the pre-Herodian surrounding wall.

The Foundation of the Brotherhood

Taking into account the information above, it may now be possible to put together a more informed description of the formation of the Knights Templar, using the work of Guillaume de Tyre and the chronicles of Fulcher of Chartres as a base to build on.

De Tyre's starting point was that in 1118, a group of nine otherwise unheard of knights, presented at the court of the king of Jerusalem, offering to protect pilgrims travelling to the Holy Land. He also stated that the strength of the order remained at nine for the next nine years. It appears that this may have been only an approximation of the actual events. The authors of 'The Holy Blood and the Holy Grail', found a letter in the 'The Recueil des Historiens des Croisades', a collection of works which has become one of the most important research documents on the crusades. The letter which was written by the bishop of Chartres in 1114, to the count of Champagne contains the passage;

'We have heard that ... before leaving for Jerusalem you made a vow to join "La malice du Christ", that you wish to enrol in this evangelical soldiery'. (The Holy Blood and The Holy Grail, Baigent, Leigh & Lincoln. Pg88).

From the context of the letter it is evident that the bishop was referring to the future Templars and as the letter was written in 1114, the organisation must have existed then. So this takes the foundation of the Templars back by more than four years. Furthermore the bishop died in 1115, so it is certain that he could not have written about an organisation, which was not formed until three years after his death.

The situation has been further confused by the discovery of a Templar archive in Seborga, northern Italy. It is stated in the document that in order to protect a great secret, Bernard of Clairvaux founded a monastery on the Italian site in 1113, where he installed two monks who had joined the Cistercian order with him, named Gondemar and Rossal. The archives also records that in February 1117, Bernard blessed the two monks, together with seven knights before they left for the Holy Land in November 1118. The seven knights who joined Gondemar and Rossal are named as; Hughes de Payen, Andre de Montbard, Hugh I Count of Champagne, Payen de Montdidier, Geoffroi de St Omer, Archambaud de St-Amand and Geoffroi Bisol. Hughes de Payen was documented also as being consecrated by Abbot Edouard of Seborga, as the first Grand master of the 'Poor Militia of Christ', under instruction from Bernard, thus dating the foundation of the order as February 1117 and the founder as Bernard of Clarvaux.

Although the precise date of the beginnings of the Templars is uncertain, it does become clear that there existed a cabal or organisation of like-minded and probably inter-related families acting behind the scenes. They structured the events leading up to the beginnings of both the Templar and the Cistercian movements; organisations which were connected at a core level. In 1104 the count of Champagne attended a secret meeting of these families, which appears to have prompted, or been in connection to, his visit to Jerusalem as he left straight after the meeting, not returning for four years. During his time back in Troyes, the count saw Bernard of Burgundy join the Cistercians in 1112, before again journeying to the Holy

The Cathar Country

Land in 1114. Whatever the reason for this visit, Hugh returned a year later and made a donation of the lands of Val d'Absinthe, for the construction of Bernard's monastery of Clairvaux. He then returned to the Temple Mount and became initiated into the Templar movement in 1124, thus disproving de Tyre's theory that the membership of the Knights Templar remained at nine for nine years. Or maybe de Tyre was referring to the knights from Seborga in his record of the events, but either way his date of formation of the order was incorrect.

Now, we turn to the activities of the nine knights after they had taken up residency in their private wing of the Royal palace, directly above the foundations of the old temple. We have already suggested that Guillaume de Tyre's story that the knights were protecting pilgrims en-route to the Holy Land, could have been a cover story, as nine knights would have very little effect protecting such vast lands. It would appear that some planning and scheming had taken place before they travelled, so they must have had a purpose. What was that purpose?

For the answer to this we have to look again at the Cohan priests of the temple and their role as protectors of the treasures, holy relics and secrets dating back through Egypt and probably to Sumaria. During the Jewish revolt against the Roman invaders the city was under siege, providing enough time for the Priests to hide the temple assets in the labyrinth of caves beneath the Temple Mount. When the Romans eventually sacked the city and destroyed the temple, they recovered a mass of riches and removed them to Rome, but they did not know of some of the secret caves, which the temple priests had blocked off and which contained a great proportion of the treasures.

The knowledge of the whereabouts of this booty would have been known to one group of people only and that would be the descendants of the priests of the temple. This would be the Rex Deus families, the very group of conspirators, including Hugh I, the Count of Champagne, Bernard of Clairvaux and the original nine Knights Templar. The group who had met at the secret conclave, before Count Hugh made his journey to the Holy Land to visit King Baldwin I of Jerusalem; another Rex Deus family member.

It would appear to be no coincidence that King Baldwin provided the early Templars with quarters above the very catacombs where the massive wealth and knowledge of their ancestors had been hidden. There exists clear evidence that the Templars spent their first nine years digging in these caves and catacombs right beneath them, in order to recover the treasures, which they would have seen as their birth right. The most conclusive evidence came as a result of excavations carried out by General Sir Charles Wilson of the British Royal Engineers, who also became the head of the London Metropolitan Police at the time of the Jack the Ripper murders. Wilson's excavations in 1867 discovered an 80 feet vertical access tunnel, through solid rock, at the bottom of which numerous horizontal tunnels fed off in several directions. Deep within these tunnels Wilson's men discovered items of Templar property, such as remnants of a lance, a spur and an almost complete Templar sword.

After this initial period of digging and recovery of the treasures, relics and ancient manuscripts hidden within the temple mount, the Templars returned to France to attend the Council of Troyes. The order now really did have something to protect and it was important for them to create a solid base of legitimacy, if they were to be free to develop into the powerful organisation they were destined to become. This was going to be the job of Bernard of Clairvaux, who had already been manoeuvred into a position of power, as a senior abbot of the Cistercian order. As discussed above, Bernard hijacked the Council of Troyes in order to provide the Templar order with a Holy Rule, the first of many papal edicts in favour of the new order.

The Growth of the Order

After the Council of Troyes, the Templars began recruiting rapidly from the ranks of the nobility and according to the rules of the order, all new knights had to hand over their possessions, except for their sword. As the order grew in strength it began possessing massive holdings of lands, castles and real-estate throughout Europe, from newly initiated knights and gifts from kings and leading families. By the mid 1130s donations were being received so rapidly that the order did not have the available man-power to take ownership and were often forced to delay occupation.

Bernard of Clairvaux was employing his first rate communication skills in a publicity campaign to rally financial support and new recruits for the rapidly expanding Templar order. He produced and distributed a pamphlet named 'de Laude Novae Militiae', or 'In Praise of the New Knighthood', spreading a message that supporting or joining the Templars would be good for your eternal soul. The tract, which appears today almost ranting, extols the Knights as paragons of the holy fight;

'A new kind of chivalry, one ignorant of the ways of the ages, which fights a double fight equally and tirelessly, both against flesh and blood and against the spiritual forces of iniquity in the heavens. When a man mightily resists a bodily foe by strength of his body alone, I no more think it a wonder than I believe it to be a rare occurence; nor is it marvelous, though I might call it praiseworthy, when a man declares war on vice or demons with the power of his soul, since the world is full of monks. But when both of these kinds of men are girded with their own particular powerful sword and distinguished with their own particular noble belt in a single man, who would not judge this, which is as yet an unfamiliar thing, to be most worthy of all admiration? He indeed is a fearless knight, and one secure from any quarter, since his soul is dressed in an armor of faith just as his body is dressed in an armor of steel. Since he is well protected by both kinds of arms, he fears neither the demon nor man. Nor is he afraid of death, since he longs to die. Why should he fear whether he lives or dies, since for him life is Christ and death is a reward?' (from - *de Laude Novae Militiae'* (1128-1131), Bernard Clairvaux).

In his book 'The Knights of the Holy Grail', Tim Wallace-Murphy points to a particularly telling sentence towards the end of Clairvaux's 'de Laude Novae Militiae', which may provide some insight into the deeper goals of the Templars and their associates'.

'Hail, land of promise, which, formerly flowing only with milk and honey for thy possessors, now stretchest forth the food of life and the means of salvation of the entire world'. (from - *de Laude Novae Militiae'* (1128-1131), Bernard Clairvaux).

The Cathar Country

Was Bernard of Clairvaux suggesting that the world had not yet been saved, which would be in total contradiction to the teaching of the Christian Church, which states that Jesus became the saviour of the world with his death on the cross? This of course would be the very heresy against which was preached, but as advisor and tutor to popes, he was in a position to influence church opinion. Another extremely powerful Rex Deus family, the Hapsburgs of Austria, have the family motto, which also seems to indicate plans for the entire world, 'Austriae est imperare orbi universo', or A.E.I.O.U. (it falls to Austria to rule over the whole globe).

As a result of Bernard of Clairvaux's marketing activities, an avalanche of gifts and new recruits flowed towards the Templars and by the time Hughes de Payen returned to the Holy Land after the Council of Troyes, he had 300 knights with him. The Cistercians established over 300 new abbeys, which was the most substantial growth of any monastic order ever. The two orders were considered as branches of the same organisation, the Templars being the fighting force and the Cistercians providing the power of prayer.

With the receipt of vast areas of lands, the Templars grew exponentially in power and they soon held large holdings in; Provence, Champagne, England, Tuscany, Aragon, Gallicia, Portugal, Scotland, Normandy, the Holy Land and Occitan in the South of France. It was here in the Languedoc that they had over 30% of their properties outside the Holy Land and it was here that they had long aimed to create a nation state of their own.

The Cathar Country

A process of administrative control was becoming essential and it was the original nine knights that were used firstly to take control of the various areas around Europe. It was Brother Hugh Rigaud who was given administrative authority over the Languedoc region. He is known to have met early after the Council of Troyes with senior members of the Trencavel family, including Roger I of Beziers and his brothers Raymond Trencavel I and Bernard Atton V, together with their mother, the Viscountess Cecily.

The Knights Templar were to become the richest most powerful organisation on the planet, with massive holdings stretching from the Baltic to the Mediterranean and from the Atlantic to the Holy Land. Through donations of mills, farmhouses, barns, chapels, commanderies and other business premises, the Templars built the first multinational conglomerate in the world. They had vast business interests including; wine and olive oil production, mining of coal and minerals, glass production, wool and cloth, metal smelting, lumber, banking, travel and through their fleet of ships, export and import of all of the above. They became massive employers of local people and tenant farmers who paid a ten percent tithe to the very Templars who had been made immune to tithes and taxes through papal bull.

The Templars went into the package tour business supplying transport and accommodation for pilgrimages travelling to; Jerusalem, Rome, Chartres, Mont St. Michel and the shrine of St. James, at Santiago de Compostela. Through their banking activities, the Templars were able to supply travellers with an early type of travellers' cheques or credit card, as a form of safe currency for their journey, which of course would be supplied at interest. A traveller would deposit a sum of money at their local Templar commanderie, they would then be given a coded chit, which could be used to withdraw money or pay bills during their journey. When they returned home they would cash in the chit, or pay the outstanding balance, at the same Temlplar establishment, who issued it.

The Templar financial services business grew into the first real bank; they lent money at interest to clients across the spectrum of society right up to kings and saved King Louis VII from financial ruin. They paid retirement pension incomes and annuities, backed by the transfer of properties and land to the Templars coffers, which resulted in a vast property portfolio. In the 12th and 13th centuries the Knight Templar owned the first European Central Bank and the in the 21st century the Rex Deus families are at the forefront of forming the second.

The Templars owned a large fleet of ships which they used to facilitate pilgrimages, overseas trade, income and exports and the transfer of knights, armoury and of course money. The fleet's primary headquarters were at La Rochelle on the Bay of Biscay on France's west coast, 300 miles from both Paris and the Languedoc and with clear access to Britain. They also held ships at ports in Portugal and around the Mediterranean. A portion of the fleet were war-ships, which carried out the first recorded acts of privateering, or attacking and pillaging enemy ships under the permission of the papacy and royalty.

By the last decade of the 13th centaury, the Templars had reached a peak of previously un-heard of success; they were more powerful than kings, countries and the church. But within the success of the Templars' banking and financial activities, lay the seeds of their eventual downfall.

Friday 13th and the end game

The beginning of the end for the Knights Templar could be traced back to the 1291 siege of the city of Acre, which lies just over 100 miles north of Jerusalem. When the city fell to the Moslems, the crusaders only held the tiny island of Ruad in the area and when that finally fell in 1302/1303 they had totally lost control of the Holy Land. This turn of events removed the main reason for the Templars existence, as their major activity, according to the papacy, had always been to protect the kingdom of Jerusalem.

In April 1293, Theobald Gaudin, who had been elected Grand Master towards the end of the siege of Acre, died leaving a vacancy at the head of an order with a now uncertain future. After a closely fought election, which had to be overseen by the Grand Master of the Knights Hospitaller, Jacques de Molay was sworn in as the 23rd Grand Master of the Knights Templar, at the new headquarters in Limassol, in Cyprus. De Molay, who had been a member of the order for some thirty years, had one objective and that was to regain control of Outremer and with the assistance of Pope Nicholas IV, he called for a new crusade to this end.

It was against this backdrop that calls for an amalgamation between the two orders of the Templars and the Hospitallers, were being heard, as it was quarrels between the two orders that were being blamed for the loss of the Holy Land. King Philippe le Bel of France had come to power in 1285 and he had become seriously in dept, mainly through the funding of various wars, in particular the war against England. He had levied stringent taxes against the lords of the Languedoc, who

The Cathar Country

were still reeling from the effects of the Albigensian Crusade and had taken forced loans from the majority of his vassals.

In an effort to get the papacy on his side, Philippe supported Bertrand de Goth, the French Archbishop of Bordeaux, who was not even a cardinal, to gain the papacy, under the name Pope Clement V. It was from this position of power that the French king was to move against the Templars, his greatest financial creditors. Pope Clement summoned the leaders of both the Templars and Hospitallers to a meeting in Paris, were they were to discuss the amalgamation of the order.

The Grand Master of the Knights Hospitaller, William de Villaret made the excuse that he was not able to leave an assault on Rhodes, but Jacques de Molay had no such diversion and he was forced to attend the meeting, which he probably knew could well be a trap. Behind the scenes Philippe le Bel had put proceedings in motion and now that he had de Molay on his territory, he sprung the ambush. At dawn on Friday 13th October 1307, the agents of the king opened sealed orders they had been holding for a month. All the Templars in France, including Jacques de Molay, were arrested under charges of heresy, sodomy, blasphemy and denying Christ.

This was not the first time that Philippe had carried out such an act; in 1303 he had failed in an attempted to arrest Pope Boniface VIII under similar charges and in 1311 he had arrested the Italian 'Lombard' bankers and seized their assets. The arrest of the Templars was seen by many of the nobility of Europe as a ruse to clear the debts of the king of France and as a chance for him get his hands on the Templar treasure.

Clement V was furious about this unilateral royal decision and worried about the very existence of the church. He wrote to the king on 27th October saying that Philip had 'violated every rule in an act of contempt towards ourselves and the Roman Church'. After confessions from the knights, received after torture, pressure on the Pope resulted in the papal bull 'Pastoralis praeeminentiae', which ordered the arrest of all Templars throughout Europe. The effects of the pope's orders were to say the least, underwhelming with mixed reactions from the kings of the countries of Europe. In an effort to rein in king Philippe, Pope Clement V organised that the Templars should be heard before a papal committee. On 24th December 1307, at this meeting Jacques de Molay and his colleagues all retracted their confessions, stating that they were obtained under torture.

After much in-fighting between the pope and the king, Clement found himself in ever increasing danger from the kings men. Eventually he gave in to pressure and allowed Philippe to take control of the trial, which eventually began on 22nd November 1309. The results of the proceedings were pre-decided; the first 54 Templars were burned alive on 12th May 1310 and soon after two papal bulls were issued, 'Vox in excelso' (22nd March 1312), which dissolved the Templar Order and 'Ad providam' (2nd May 1312), which confounded Philippe by transferring all the Templars property to the Hospitallers.

On Monday 18th March 1314 Jacques de Molay was brought out onto a platform outside the west front of Notre Dame de Paris, to hear the charges against him, read out by the Archbishop of Sens. De Molay had been in solitary confinement and had faced the worst that the inquisition had

The Cathar Country

to give for seven years; he was now 70 years old, with his life as a warrior knight behind him. But he took this opportunity to speak for himself and the order, which had been his family for nearly 50 years in a speech that is etched into history;

'It is just that, in so terrible a day, and in the last moments of my life, I should discover all the iniquity of falsehood, and make the truth triumph. I declare, then, in the face of heaven and earth, and acknowledge, through to my eternal shame, that I have committed the greatest of crimes but... it has been the acknowledging of those which have been so foully charged on the order. I attest – and truth obliges me to attest – that it is innocent! I made the contrary declaration only to suspend the excessive pains of torture, and to mollify those who made me endure them. I know the punishments which have been inflicted on all the knights who had the courage to revoke a similar confession; but the dreadful spectacle which is presented to me is not able to make me confirm one lie by another. The life offered me on such infamous terms I abandon without regret'. (Hopkins, Simmans, & Wallace-Murphy, *Rex Deus*).

As the crowd roared its appreciation to the moving words of Jacques de Molay, his fellow knight Geoffroi de Carney, moved to stand with his Grand Master and added his words and in a similar vein revoked his own confession. The knights were burned to death that evening on the ancient Isle des Javiaux, in Paris, where a smokeless fire was built so that the pain would be drawn out as long as possible. De Moley and de Carney were slowly cooked to death before being placed onto the fire. Before he died, legend tells of how de Molay cursed Pope Clement V and King Philippe le Bel, calling upon them both to appear before God in heaven within the year. The pope died on the 20th April and the king died on 29th November of the same year. A whole 479 years later on the

21st January 1793 another French king, Louis XVI, was led to the guillotine on Paris's Place de la Concord. The execution took place at 10.15am and as the king's head was held up before the crowd, a man leaped onto the platform, dipped his fingers into the kings blood, held his hand high and shouted 'Jacques de Moley, thus you are revenged'.

If Philippe le Bel was hoping to get hold of the templar riches, he was to be disappointed, by the time the Paris Temple was raided all the money and valuables had been removed. It is clear that the Templars had been forewarned of the orders to arrest them and the treasure had been sent by barge, out of Paris to the coast at La Rochelle, where it had been loaded onto the Templar ships. Again when the king's men reached the dock at La Rochelle, the Templar fleet had totally disappeared and it has not been seen again to this day. Jacques de Molay had also had all the order's rule books and account books burned before the arrests so the king had no paper trail to follow. The amount of money that disappeared with the Templars can not now be known, but we know that they represented the assets of a truly international bank.

The Swiss Banking Connection

In 1291 king Rudolf of Habsburg died leaving a power gap in the area of the Alps, we now know as Switzerland. At this time a new trade route was developing over St. Gotthard pass and in three small valleys which had remained outside the focus of the dukes and kings. The people of these newly formed lands of Uri, Schwyz and Unterwalden were concerned that the Hapsburgs would subject them as part of their growing empire and they were trying to avoid this and to

The Cathar Country

become an independent state. To this end the Swiss Confederation was formed on August, 1st 1291. The new confederation soon grew a massive army out of nowhere, which maintained the independence of the area until 1515 and oversaw the building of the Swiss banking system.

In the same year of 1291, the loss of Acre resulted in the Knights Templars losing the main reason for their existence, which was the protection of the Kingdom of Jerusalem. The Templars were looking for an independent homeland and their favourite venue of the Languedoc was receiving continued negative attention from the Roman Church and the French state. Through their extensive trading activities, the Templars would have known of the pass over St. Gotthard and this new area would have appeared extremely attractive as a base to build a domicile.

Local folk-lore, in the area of St. Gotthard, tells of how white clad knights' appeared and assisted in the fight to retain independence. In 1307, it is highly possible that this trade route was used to secrete the treasure out of France, together with the personnel, who had the expertise, experience and clients to form an international banking organisation. It is possible that the 'International Templar Bank' merely relocated their business premises to Switzerland in 1307. A comparison of the Templar flag, a red cross on a white background and the Swiss flag, a white cross on a red background maybe reveals the occult practice of reversing or making opposite, providing evidence that the Templars are still around in Switzerland, for those who have the eyes to see.

The Bruce and Bannockburn

Another well written about and evidenced escape route was to the west coast of Scotland; the home of some of the very families who were at the beginning of the Templar story, such as the St. Clairs of Rosslyn. At the time Scotland was in the middle of a civil war against the English crown. Robert the Bruce, the leader of the Scottish uprising had fallen out with the Roman Church because of an incident in 1306, when he had stabbed John Comyn, his rival for the throne, in a church in Dumfries. The Pope issued a papal decree against Bruce, but as this was mainly ignored in Scotland, his followers were excommunicated and when this was also ignored the pope excommunicated the whole of the country.

This mutual enemy of the Catholic Church created a safe haven for the Templars already stationed in Scotland and for those in England who headed north and for the Templar fleet, which landed around the Kintyre Peninsula area. In June 1314, the presence of the Templars is evidenced behind the scenes, when at the Battle of Bannockburn, the armies of Robert the Bruce, defeated Edward II's vastly larger English army. This unusual and unexpected defeat, which re-created an independent Scottish monarchy, must have had assistance from the new population of Knights Templars, who would have brought with them the best and most experienced fighting men in Europe, if not the world. After all how could the Templars refuse help, or even stand by and watch their new countrymen, who had given them a place of asylum, face an almost assured defeat, which would have placed them firmly back under control of the church.

The Cathar Country

Tim Wallace-Murphy made the following definite connection between the Battle of Bannockburn and the knights Templar;

'At the Battle of Bannockburn that finally secured the throne for the Bruce and completely vanquished the English invader, 432 Templar Knights (including Sir Henry St. Clair, Baron of Roslin, and his sons William and Henry) took part in the final charge which completely routed the English army and preserved Scottish independence. Rex Deus tradition recounts that after Bannockburn, as an act of gratitude and recognition, King Robert the Bruce became the sovereign Grandmaster of the Templar Order'. (Wallice-Murphy, Tim, *The Knights of the Holy Grail*).

It was not long until Robert the Bruce had to restore relations with the Vatican and communications between the papacy and the country of Scotland were re-instigated. It was at this time that the Templars disappeared from sight in Scotland, following the example of their fellow knights around Europe by going underground and fading into history, myth and legend.

Chapter 9

The Priory of Sion

It is never long after entering the world of the Rennes-le-Château mystery before you encounter the Priory of Sion. This enigmatic secret society winds its way inextricably through the story, showing its self here and there, but always remaining just out of reach. It is clear that such an organisation existed in France in 1956 and was associated with Pierre Plantard and that this same gentleman directly influenced the writings of Gérard de Sède in the 1960s and later, the work of Henry Lincoln.

Evidence also exists of a society in the 11th century, with a very similar name; which may have had an influence on the formation of the Knights Templar and with a possible connection to the Cistercian movement. Whether the relationship between the two societies goes further than a name; remains a matter of conjecture and the focus of a debate which may never be satisfied.

What is evident is that the Priory of Sion that showed its hand in the 1950s had an agenda to follow. Having forwarded this agenda this organisation may then have purposely discredited itself before evaporating underground.

The New Priory

In accordance with French law the Prior of Sion registered its existence on 7th May 1956 in the town of Saint-Julien-en-Genevois, on the outskirts of Geneva and the event was recorded in the weekly publication 'Journal Officiel de la République Française', on 20th July. The group recorded its headquarters as being located in Annemasse, which is also around 6 miles from Geneva and its officers as; André Bonhomme (Stanis Bellas), as President, Jean Delaval, Vice-President, Armand Defago, Treasurer and Pierre Plantard (Chyren), as Secretary General.

This form of the organisation, who's stated aims could be described as a mixture of Catholic 'good works' and Masonic brotherhood, was fated to last less than a year, but Pierre Plantard oversaw the formation of a similar order in 1961, which lasted 23 years.

Plantard was born in Paris on 18th March 1920, just three years after the death of Bérenger Saunière. With an almost aristocratic manner, he spoke of being the son of the Compt de Saint Clair and Compt de Rhedae and he had a birth certificate to prove it. When Henry Lincoln produced a copy of a similar document stating that Plantard was the son of a butler, he was ready with the answer that this certificate had been produced to put the German invaders off his trail. During WWII whilst still in his early 20s, Plantard began an organisation called 'Alpha Galates' (The First Gauls), which again only lasted around six months as he was arrested by the German authorities and imprisoned for four months in Paris, as a direct result of his pro-French activities. It is possible that

The Cathar Country

Plantard spent the immediate post-war years working in Switzerland at the invitation of the Swiss government, before returning to Annemasse on the French side of the border around 1956, to work as a draughtsman.

By 1961 Plantard had taken to the habit of lodging his writings in the Bibliotheque Nationale, beginning with his paper 'Gisors et son secret' (Gisors and its secrets). Around the same time a certain collection of documents was also deposited in the library in instalments and under assumed names. These papers had been prepared by Plantard and his friend Philippe de Cherisey, a marquis from the Lorraine region, who had taken up a career as a writer, radio humourist and actor. Out of this collection of fifteen documents, which together build up a story centred around Rennes-le-Château and the Priory of Sion; the following five are of the most significance;

The **'Genealogy of the Merovingian Kings'**, was deposited in the Bibliotheque Nationale in 1964 under the authorship of Henri Lobineau (Pierre Plantard). They comprise mainly of a carefully and elaborately drawn out set of genealogical tables, tracing the line of the Merovingian dynasty from Merovee, King of the Franks from 451 to 458, through Dagobert I and up to the seventeenth century. Napoleon was fascinated by the Merovingians and commissioned their genealogies to be compiled in order to find out whether the dynasty had survived after it was deposed. It is possible that these Napoleonic documents were used as a background for the Lobineau papers, but with an added heredity link to the Plantard family.

'A Merovingian Treasure at Rennes-le-Chateau', was deposited on 13th May 1966 and attributed to Antoine l'Ermite (probably Philippe de Cherisey). This was a short ten page pamphlet mainly repeating the Rennes-le-Château story, as told by Noel Corbu, the owner of the Saunière domaine and the Hotel de la Tour, to enthral his guests.

'Engraved stones of the Languedoc', was deposited on 20th June 1966, again by Henri l'Ermite and it contained a selection of drawings by Gerard de Sade, supposedly from a book by Eugene Stublien. It is not at all certain whether this book ever existed, but a grave baring the name Stublien can be found in Alet-les-Bains churchyard, which at least provides evidence that the family lived in the area.

'Le Serpent Rouge', is a small collection of genealogical lists and old French maps, together with thirteen short poems, each ascribed to a sign of the zodiac, including the thirteenth sign Ophiuchus. These unfathomable verses, which refer to the church at Rennes-le-Château and the surrounding area, have been the source of much speculation and have produced many theories about the mystery. Although 'Le Serpent Rouge', or the Red Snake, had clearly been written by de Cherisey, perhaps its strangest aspect is the ascribing of its authorship to three men who had all recently committed suicide. Pierre Fougere, Louis Saint-Maxent and Gaston de Koker, all hanged themselves around 7th March 1967 and thus provided names which can not be confirmed. It is also uncertain why the article needed three authors. The document found it's way into the library on 20th March 1967, but the date given for writing it was the infamous January 17th, the date of the death of Mary de Blanchefort and so many other incidents, covered in chapter 5 above, including the feast day of St Sulpice and a ground plan of this church is included in Le Serpent Rouge.

'The Secret File of Henri Lobineau'; deposited in 1967, could be described as a scrap book rounding up the work of Henri Lobineau, with the usual genealogical manuscripts, maps and stories about the Merovingians and their connection to Rennes-le-Château and the Priory of Sion. This work also provides a cover story for Lobineau's death in an attempt to fend off unhelpful questions as to his background and history. Papers in the file state that Lobineau was actually one Leo Schidlof, who had died in 1966 and so would not be available for questioning on the matter.

Having planted the documents into the library, it was time to feed them with the nutrient of publicity. This was to be the job firstly of Gerard de Sade, who brought the story to France and then Henry Lincoln, who was largely responsible for spreading the story outside France and to the English speaking world.

It is whilst he was living in Annemasse that Plantard became an associate of Gerard de Sade, who shared his interest in the occult and in particular its connection to the Knight Templars and events surrounding the story of Rennes-le-Château. Plantard provided an extensive appendix for de Sade's 1962 book 'Les Templiers sont parmi nous' (The Templars are among us), which introduced the concept of the Priory of Sion. It also pointed de Sade in the general direction of the Bibliotheque Nationale and the strange collection of papers to be found concerning the Merovingian bloodline, Rennes-le-Château and the Priory of Sion. Having researched the Secret Papers, de Sade reproduced much of the information in his book 'L'Or de Rennes', ('Le Trésor Maudit de Rennes-le-Château', in paperback) in 1967 and as a result, the names of

The Cathar Country

Saunière, Rennes-le-Château and the Priory of Sion became household names in France.

Then in 1969 the English actor and screen writer, Henry Lincoln joined the stage. As he tells the story; he came across a copy of de Sade's book, whilst on holiday in the Languedoc and became fascinated with the hidden codes and half concealed messages, he began to uncover from the pages of the book. The following year he met Gerard de Sade in Paris, as part of the research, which resulted in three BBC films on the subject. This produced a flood of interest in the Rennes-le-Château mystery, which turned into a torrent, after the publication of Lincoln, Baigent and Leigh's best seller, 'Holy Blood and the Holy Grail', in 1982.

After much investigation and with the benefit of a constant trickle of so called secret documents from the Plantard camp, Lincoln and his co-authors came to the conclusion that the Priory of Sion still exists. They found that it had become an extensive organisation with a pyramidal hierarchical structure headed by the Grand Master or 'Nautonnier' and with a membership that had grown from around 1,093 in 1956, up to around 9,841 at the time of their research.

'The Priory of Sion exists today and is still operative. It is influential and plays a role in high-level international affairs, as well as in the domestic affairs of certain European countries. To some significant extent it is responsible for the body of information disseminated since 1956. The avowed and declared objective of the Priory of Sion is the restoration of the Merovingian dynasty and bloodline – to the throne not only of France, but to the thrones of other European nations as well. The restoration of the Merovingian dynasty is sanctioned and justifiable, both legally and morally.

Although deposed in the eighth century, the Merovingians bloodline did not become extinct. On the contrary it perpetuated itself in a direct line from Dagobert II and his son, Sigisbert IV. By dint of dynastic alliances and intermarriages, this line came to include Godfroi de Bouillon, who captured Jerusalem in 1099 and various other nobles and royal families, past and present – Blanchefort, Gisors, Saint-Clair (Sinclair in England), Montesquiou, Montpezat, Poher, Lusignan, Plantard and Hapsburg-Lorraine. At present, the Merovingian bloodline enjoys a legitimate claim to its rightful heritage'. (Baigent, Leigh and Lincoln, The Holy Blood and the Holy Grail, Pg 108/109)

An Ancient Order

Legend has it that the origins of the Priory of Sion can be traced back to the ancient Egyptian city of Alexandria, where the occult adept, Ormus (Ormesius in Greek), is said to have started the secret society, the 'Ordo Ormesius'. Ormus, who was a priest of Serapis, foreseeing the approach of Christianity decided the best way to preserve the 'old ways' was to openly convert to the new religion, which he did in AD 44. In this way he was able to secretly and safely continue his initiatory magical practices underground, a mode of operation followed by members of similar organisations down through history. The Ordo Ormesius is thought by many to have developed into the 'Order of Zion' and to have spawned many Hermetic societies such as the Golden Dawn.

After the conquest of Jerusalem it became necessary to decide on a suitable monarch to rule over the Holy Land and at a secret council it was decided that Godfroi de Bouillon would take on the role. Considering the future treatment by the

Catholic Church, it is somewhat revealing that Raymond Roger of Toulouse, was also considered for the position.

'A secret Jewish order was behind these men, the Order of Zion (l'Ordre de Sion), founded in the monastery of Notre-Dame du Mont de Sion, on mount Zion, just south of Jerusalem, in June 1099 by the 39 year-old Godfroi de Bouillon, duke of Lorraine - a descendant of Guillem de Gellone, who was of the seed and tribe of David. The first grand master of the order was Hughes de Payens, who later founded the Knights Templar. Another member was Andre de Montbard. The original name was Chevaliers de l'Ordre de Notre-Dame de Sion'. (Lina, Juri, *Architects of Deception*, Pg 33)

Having set up the Knights Templar under the leadership of Hughes de Payen twenty or so years later, from their headquarters at the Abbey of Notre Dame on Mont Sion, just south of Jerusalem, the order was forced to withdraw to France in 1187, when the Holy-Land was lost to Saladin's Islamic armies. During these early years the Order of Sion and the Order of the Temple are thought to have had extremely close ties and to have even shared the same Grand Master. But on returning to France the name 'Priory of Sion', is recorded for the first time, as the order took on a new Grand Master, Jean de Gisors. The leaders of the Priory of Sion placed the blame for the loss of Jerusalem and their resulting eviction from the Holy Land, firmly in the lap of the Grand Master, Gerard de Ridefort and they took the drastic action of separating from the Templars.

The official divorce took place in 1188 in a meadow adjacent to Château Gisors, called Champ Sacre (the sacred field), which had been used historically as a place of parley for the royals of France and England, at times of war. In the centre of the field grew a famous old elm tree, which had been used by kings and Lords, down through history as a meeting place and it was here that the separation of the orders took place at a ceremony known as the 'Cutting of the Elm'.

According to the Dossiers Secrets, since their separation from the Templars, the Prior of Sion has survived the tragic disbanding of their sister order in 1307. They have continued to take part in major world events behind the scenes, under the leadership of the following Grand Masters, which include some of Europe's most illustrious names;

Jean de Gisors (1188-1220)
Marie de Saint-Clair (1220-1266)
Guillaume de Gisors (1266-1307)
Edouard de Bar (1307-1336)
Jeanne de Bar (1336-1351)
Jean de Saint-Clair (1351-1366)
Blanche d'Evreux (1366-1398)
Nicolas Flamel (1398-1418)
René d'Anjou (1418-1480)
Iolande de Bar (1480-1483)
Sandro Filipepi (1483-1510)
Léonard de Vinci (1510-1519)
Connétable de Bourbon (1519-1527)
Ferdinand de Gonzague (1527-1575)
Louis de Nevers (1575-1595)
Robert Fludd (1595-1637)
J. Valentin Andrea (1637-1654)
Robert Boyle (1654-1691)
Isaac Newton (1691-1727)
Charles Radclyffe (1727-1746)
Charles de Lorraine (1746-1780)

The Cathar Country

Maximilian de Lorraine (1780–1801)
Charles Nodier (1801–1844)
Victor Hugo (1844–1885)
Claude Debussy (1885–1918)
Jean Cocteau (1918–1963)

A Continuing Order?

Evidence of the early existence of the Priory of Sion is thin on ground, as would be expected of a society set up to be secret and to operate in the dark and behind closed doors. It is therefore difficult to investigate by nature and although many researchers have come up with little for their efforts, it is still Baigent, Leigh and Lincoln, that lead the field. These authors state that they base their work mainly on information fed to them by Pierre Plantard, Henri de Cherisey and to some extent, Gerard de Sade. It is up to the individual to decide for themselves, based on the information available, but the backgrounds, elegancies and motives of all the players in this game, if taken at face value, could be misleading, 'Caveat Emotor', let the 'buyer be aware'!

'There was a secret order behind the Knights Templar, which created the Templars as its military and administrative arm. This order, which has functioned under a variety of names, is most frequently known as the Prieure de Sion ('Priory of Sion'). The Priory of Sion has been directed by a sequence of Grand Masters whose names are amongst the most illustrious in Western history and culture. Although the Knights Templar were destroyed and dissolved between 1307 and 1314, the Prieure de Sion remained unscathed. Although itself periodically torn by internecine and factional strife, it has continued to function through the centuries. Acting in the shadows, behind the scenes, it has orchestrated certain of the critical events in

The Cathar Country

Western history'. (Baigent, Leigh and Lincoln, *The Holy Blood and the Holy Grail,* Pg 108/109)

The Knights Templar clearly existed, as did the Cistercian Order and evidence for the existence of the Rex Deus families is overwhelming. So how difficult is it to believe that a further organisation would exist, with a mandate of overseeing their ancient heritage and directing future events in line with their age old goals. It is clear that an immense amount of work went into the preparation of the documents deposited in the Bibliotheque Nationale. The meticulous preparation of whole genealogies, the elaborately drawn out documents and maps, the writing of coded poems and the working out of intricate coding, must have taken months, if not years, to complete. Would Plantard really do all this just to raise a low self esteem, as suggested by some writers? De Cherisey certainly had no need for this elevation of status; he was born a marquis of the same Lower Lorraine as Godfroi de Bouillon. So why was all this effort necessary, what was the desired result?

If a secret organisation has to temporarily show its existence in order to achieve an intermediary goal, it is an easy thing for it to purposefully discredit itself and disappear again unsearched for. An arbitrary explanation of any strange event or happening is readily accepted by the mass of the population, who are more than happy to be provided with an excuse not to look further into the matter, an activity which can be disturbing to the easy running of the daily routine. Every summer in the rolling fields of Wiltshire, dozens of intricately designed Crop-Circles appear over night to the amazement of locals and visitors, so the media produced the story of Doug Bower and Dave Chorley, who told of how they made them all using planks and ropes. This was enough for the majority people and the mystery was apparently solved. The incidence of UFO sighting reports has leaped massively in the last decade, but these are put down to flying Chinese lanterns and as for ghosts and other related phenomenon, we are told from birth that there is no such thing.

Equally many researchers into the Rennes-le-Château mystery are happy to write off the Priory of Sion, as the grandiose dream of Pierre Plantard, whose nefarious background was proved by his having served six months in prison in 1953 over allegations relating to fraud and embezzlement. But it can not be argued that the Priory of Sion has added greatly to the mystery of Rennes-le-Château and that if it was the intention to leak out a message, then that goal was overwhelmingly achieved. Much of the mystery involves content, which would have put the sender in direct conflict with the Vatican, a situation which in previous generations would have resulted in the most horrific of deaths, as thousands of Cathars and then the Knights Templar, discovered to their peril.

Into the Future

Many researchers into historical world events, some more controversial than others, have looked into the activities of the Priory of Sion and its possible effects and have come to the conclusion that the organisation is active on the global political stage, as an unseen hand of influence;

'The Prieure de Sion initiated with the aid of the moneychangers (above all the Portuguese rabbi Menasseh ben Israel, who lived in the Netherlands, and Antonio Fernandez Moses Carvajal) the insurrection of 1642, led by Oliver Cromwell, which in turn led to

the first republic (commonwealth) in England in 1649.' (Lina, Juri, *Architects of Deception*, Pg 138)

'In November of 1688 (under the sign of Scorpio), the catholic king of England James II (Stuart) was overthrown through an well organized invasion financed by the moneyed Jews of Amsterdam and led by the Prieure de Sion and the Orange Order. The king was exiled to France and in February of 1689 William of Orange, the prince of Nassau, was put upon the English throne by means of a coup d'etat, which became known as the Glorious Revolution. Even official historians admit that the people did not participate in this coup'. (Lina, Juri, *Architects of Deception*, Pg 139)

'Father George (Bush) and wife Barbara are both decedents of Godfroi de Bouillon who, in 1099, led European noblemen in the successful Crusade to recapture Jerusalem from the Islamic faith and moved into the King's palace at Temple Mount... Godfroi de Boullion was the first King of Jerusalem and the Duke of Lower Lorraine, a major region for the Illuminati bloodline... So when George W. Bush, a descendent of de Bouillon through his mother and father, talked of a "crusade" against "Islamic" terrorism... this was no slip of the tongue'. (Icke, David, Alice In Wonderland and the WTC Disaster)

'Researchers into the history and influence of the Order of Sion have established the fact that it instigated what is known as the "Scottish Rite" Freemasonic system prevalent in the United States of America. Agents of the order, such as Chevalier Ramsey and Albert Pike, were very active propagators of the "Scottish Rite" systems and practices, those which for all their mystique are merely vehicles carrying forth a very old and insidious agenda'. (Tsarion, Michael, The Irish Origins of Civilisation, Pg 704).

Chapter 10

The Nazis, 'Indiana Jones' and the Temple of Solomon

The Second World War was still five years in the future when in 1934 SS-Reichsführer Heinrich Himmler chose Wewelsburg Castle, in central Germany's Alma valley, as the headquarters of the SS and the Camelot for his quest for the Holy Grail. The location of the stronghold was fundamental in its selection as the nearby Teutoburg Forest was the site of a gigantic battle in 9AD, where the Gemanic tribes defeated the Roman legions of Varus, creating a border between the Roman Empire and Germania. This celebrated victory, which established the Teutonic Knights place in history, became the centre of the Nazi mindset of Aryan superiority. Himmler considered himself to be a King Arthur figure, heading an order of warrior monks, following in the tradition of the Teutonic knights, the Knights of the Round Table and the Knights Templar.

SS-Reichsführer Heinrich Himmler

Once a year the secret inner order of twelve member knights, chosen from the senior ranks of the SS Gruppenführers, would meet at Wewelsburg where they each sat in a grand armchair with an engraved silver nameplate, around an Arthurian style oaken round table. They also had their coats-of-arms on the walls behind their position and beneath the table a circular well called the 'realm of the dead', would be used to ritually cremate the coats of arms after the knights had died. Each knight had a personal room dedicated to an ancestor from Aryan history, Himmler himself had a chamber devoted to the

The Cathar Country

Saxon King Henry the Fowler, king of the Germans from 919 to 937 AD.

In July 1935, the year after setting up his nest of operations at Wewelsburg, Himmler's deep interest in the occult, led him to take control of the 'Ahnenerbe Forschungs-und Lehrgemeinschaft', or 'Ancestral Heritage Research and Teaching Society'. In April 1940 he incorporated the unit into the SS under his personal control at the castle. The SS Ahnenerbe travelled the world in search of early routes of Aryan civilisation and occult secrets and it was not long before they turned their attention to the Languedoc and the treasures of Solomon's temple.

Wewelsburg Castle

The work of the German researcher and author Otto Wilhelm Rahn (1904 – 1939) had come to Himmler's attention. In his book 'Crusade Against the Grail', Rahn speaks in great length about his love for the Languedoc and the ideology of the

Cathars, of which he was in nearly total philosophical agreement. His fondness for the romantic times of the troubadours and poets of the courts of the Trencavel, the Toulouse and the Foix dynasties flows from the pages of his work. Of particular interest to the Reichsführer, was Rahn's in depth study of the history of the Languedoc, leading up to the Albigensian crusade of the 13th century and its association with 'Parsifal'. Rahn makes convincing comparisons between real places and people and some of those found in Parsifal, including the location of the Holy Grail in a cave near a castle called Montsalvat, which he identified as Montségur.

Otto Rahn

In 1936 Rahn received a letter from Himmler, containing what Francis Ford Coppola's, Don Corleone would have called 'an offer he could not refuse'. Having been offered a position in

The Cathar Country

the SS by the Reichsführer himself, he really was not in a position to decline. He was initiated into the SS on 12th March 1936 as private and proceeded to fly through the ranks, making 1st Lieutenant by 11th September 1938, with special duties as personal advisor to Himmler on occult matters. Rahn did not have the heart of a natural Nazi and on 9th June 1938 he asked for extended leave to concentrate on writing a sequel to his book 'Lucifer's Courtiers', which had become the Nazi occult bible. This could well have been an attempt to pull him-self away from a regime, which was alien to his personality and philosophy and was heading in a direction he just could not be part of. He then made the mistake of allowing his opposition to the coming war be publicly known, which to his adopted masters, was not an acceptable policy. To make matters worse, on 28th February 1939 he resigned his commission and less than a month later way found dead, frozen on an Austrian mountainside. The official cause of death was suicide; however this was never proved and it remains the source of much speculation.

The story of Otto Rahn lives on today through Hollywood, as the inspiration for Steven Spielberg's 'Indiana Jones'. Spielberg's films are known for following the difficult story lines of true characters and in 1993 he released 'Schindler's List', another story connected with the atrocities of the SS.

The Cathar Country

Otto Skorzeny

By the time of Rahn's death, Himmler would have thoroughly extracted all of his occult knowledge and the Nazi quest for the Holy Grail continued under a new champion, by the name of SS Standartenfuehrer, Otto Skorzeny, or 'The Scar', as he was known after the results of a duelling accident. The six feet four inch tall Skorzeny had distinguished himself in September 1943, with the daring glider rescue of Mussolini from a mountain-top hotel, to position him as Hitler's puppet leader of Italy. The story of Skorzeny's escapades in the Languedoc were recorded by, Colonel Howard A, Buechner, whose excellent credentials have been succinctly recorded by the American researcher, journalist and author, Jim Mars.

'A native of New Orleans, Howard A. Buechner earned a bachelor's degree from Tulane University and a medical degree from Louisiana State University. During World War II, Dr Buechner was a medical

The Cathar Country

officer with the 3rd Battalion, 157th Infantry Regiment of the 45th Division, the unit that arrived first at Dachau concentration camp. Dr Buechner was the first American physician to enter the camp upon its liberation. He was later promoted to colonel while serving in the post-war reserves. It was during his wartime experiences, on the scene, that Colonel Buechner first learned of the loss of Solomon's treasure. Buechner's awards included the Medical Combat Badge, the Bronze Star, three battle stars, the Army Commendation Medal, the War Cross, and the Distinguished Service Cross of Louisiana. He also became a professor of medicine at Tulane and served as emeritus professor of medicine at LSU, where an honorary professorship was established in his name. His papers on tuberculosis and other lung diseases made him an internationally recognized expert'. (Marrs, Jim, *The Rise of the Fourth Reich.* p105)

It was in March 1944, exactly seven hundred years since the fall of Montségur to the Catholic armies of Clement V, that Skorzeny's military units arrived in the Pyrenees Mountains of Southern France. Hitler and Himmler had been following occult practices to support their efforts to reintroduce the Aryan bloodline supremacy, as they would have seen it, or to us, World War II. But by the end of 1943, things were not going the way of the Nazis and they believed that the discovery of the artefacts of Solomon's Temple, including the Grail Chalice, the Ark of the Covenant and many occult manuscripts, would provide the magical key to tip the balance in their direction. Himmler was convinced that Rahn had found the hiding place of the treasure of the Cathars and that a concerted effort on the part of Skorzeny, would recover the booty for the occult purposes of the Nazi SS.

Skorzeny followed the example of the Pope's men, led by Hugues des Arcis the seneschal of Carcassonne, so many years before and under such different circumstances. They made their camp at the base of the mighty Mountain of St. Bartholomew with Montségur sitting high on its summit. This time the aim was not to lay siege and to murder the inhabitants and extinguish their peaceful way of life, but to complete the job by removing the treasure and ancient knowledge the Cathars had left behind.

After exploring the citadel remains, the Nazi scouts widened their search into the surrounding hills and came up with the first of a series of remarkable discoveries. A hidden worn out stone stairway was uncovered leading from Montségur down the mountain, providing the answer to the riddle of how the Cathar Prefects secreted artefacts through the siege in 1244. This provided Skorzeny with a start point to the trail of the treasure and he set his men on a systemized search of the area, taking into account that the most obvious places would have already been tried by his predecessor, Otto Rahn. They found an ancient escape route and followed the trail leading through the mountains to a grotto hide-out and then to a spoulga or fortified cave near the crest of Mount La Peyre, were their search came to a successful completion.

It was March 15th 1944. At day break the following morning it would be seven hundred years since the end of the two week truce between the Cathars and the siege leaders. Exactly Seven centuries since 220 Cathars walked down the mountain from Montségur to their death, at the place now occupied by the Nazi SS. It was at this time that Skorzeny sent a telegram to his leaders in Germany saying just – 'Ureka'. Signed 'Scar' - or ('Eureka, I've found it', signed in his nick-name, Scar). He

The Cathar Country

had found the treasure of Solomon. The reply came 'Well done. Congratulations. Watch the sky tomorrow at noon. Await our arrival'. Signed 'Reichsfuehrer SS'.

The following day, under the gaze of a large group of locals, gathered to remember their Cathar ancestors on this special anniversary of their brave sacrifice, a light aircraft bearing German markings flew over Montségur and formed a huge Celtic-Cross in skywriting smoke. Of course they had no idea that this signified the discovery of the ancient treasure and that it was about to be stolen. In his book 'Emerald Cup - Ark of Gold', Colonel Buechner reported the haul from the cave to have included:-

1. Thousands of gold coins...
2. Items which were believed to have come from the Temple of Solomon, which included the gold plates and fragments of wood which had once made up the Ark of Moses... a gold plated table, a candelabra with seven branches, a golden urn, a staff, a harp, a sword, innumerable golden plates and vessels, many small bells of gold and a number of precious jewels and onyx stones, some of which bore inscriptions...
3. Twelve stone tablets bearing pre-runic inscriptions which none of the experts were able to read. These items comprised the stone Grail of the Germans and of Otto Rahn.
4. A beautiful silvery Cup with an emerald-like base made of what appeared to be jasper. Three gold plaques on the Cup were inscribed with cuneiform script in an ancient language.
5. A large number of religious objects of various types... crosses from different periods which were of gold or silver and adorned with pearls and precious stones.
6. Precious stones in abundance in all shapes and sizes.
(Buechner, Howard, Emerald Cup - Ark of Gold)

By the summer of 1944 the war was not going well for the Nazis and the major players were thinking of a strategy to ensure the continuity of the regime. If the tide was to turn irrevocably against them, they needed an escape route out of Germany and the public view, for themselves and their colleagues. The one thing they did have in their favour was huge wealth. Not only did they have the treasure of the ages handed down and added to from the beginnings of time through Solomon to the Cathars, but they had also been looting Europe and Africa throughout the war. In preparation for the post war years they had melted down gold and silver into ingots and set about hiding it around the world. An example of the vast size of the treasure can be found in the small haul discovered by General George Patton's 3rd US Army, when they uncovered a fortune, mainly in gold, worth around £155,000,000 in the Merkers salt mines. The treasure recovered from Montsegur alone was estimated by Colonel Buechner to be well in excess of £36 Billion. The disappearance of the Nazi fortune, which must have totalled into the multi trillions, was listed by the 'Guinness Book of World Records' as 'the largest robbery in the history of the world'.

Hitler's deputy, Martin Bormann had taken over the reins of power as the leader had become increasingly under the influence of prescription amphetamines and reality had all but deserted him. Bormann was running not only the Nazis and the National Socialist Party, but he had also taken a firm grip on the German economy. He called a meeting to bring together the heads of German business, banking and industry, at the Hotel Maison Rouge, in Strasbourg, to organise the continuity of National Socialism into peace-time, whilst increasing the profitability of the party's' investments. As a result of this unique summit, 'Aktion Adlerflung', or 'Operation Eagle Flight' was launched, which was a strategy for the distribution and of the Nazi wealth throughout the world.

As Bormann prepared his escape to South America, his consortium set about creating over 750 companies, to add to the 700 already created through the Swiss banking system. They were to hide the true ownership of these companies by changing names, confusing paper-trails and inserting puppet chairmen, who would run the companies for the true owners who controlled through unanimous share certificates and barer-bonds. The National Socialists were going underground. As Curtis Reiss put it;

'Everyone worked feverishly. They had better means for preparing to go underground than any other potential underground movement in the entire previous history of the world. They had all the machinery of the well-organized Nazi state. And they had a great deal of time to prepare everything. They worked very hard, but they did nothing hastily, left nothing to chance. Everything was thought through logically and organized to the last detail. Himmler planned with the utmost coolness. He chose for the work only the best-qualified experts-the best qualified, that is, in matters of underground work'. (Reiss, Curtis, *The Nazis Go Underground*, pg2)

The Nazi financial and administrational systems disappeared from sight, together with the massive wealth and resources that had waged war against half the world. This left the matter of secreting away the members of the Nazi staff, who were not regarded as disposable. At the same time that Eagle Flight was in full flow, operation ODESSA was set up to take care of this side of the underground future of the National Socialist movement. The 'Organization der ehemaligen SS-Angehorighen', or 'Organisation of former SS members', was headed up by our old friend Otto Skorzeny and was chief amongst the so called 'Rat Lines', filtering Nazi and SS personnel out of Germany and distributing them under new identities throughout the world.

It is clear that Germany lost the war in a military defeat in the summer of 1945, but it could be said that the Nazis won. The National Socialist movement is now one of the most powerful economic strengths on the planet, with its personnel intact and with business and therefore political tentacles stretching around the globe, within governments, banking and the media amongst their peacetime arsenal. Today you won't see the mass marches and rallies of Hitler's 1930s, but Nazism marches on unseen in the corridors of power. The sound of the jackboot can not be heard today above the calls for even more control of the people, but for those who have the courage to see, the results are all around us in our every day lives.

On the final page of his book Curtis Reiss wrote this warning as early as 1944;

'It is not the relative strengths of the different powers that must change, but the relations of the human beings within all the countries of this world. Some call it revolution. Some call it a new order. Whatever we call it, it must come about. If it does not, the Nazi underground will live and flourish. In due time it will make itself felt far beyond the borders of Germany. It will certainly make itself felt in this country — and no ocean will be broad enough to stop it. For Nazism or Fascism is by no means an Italian or German specialty. It is as international as murder, as greed for power, as

The Cathar Country

injustice, as madness. In our time these horrors were translated into political and cultural actuality in Italy and in Germany first. The next time . . . If we don't stamp out the Nazi underground, it will make itself felt all over the world; in this country too. We may not have to wait ten years, perhaps not even five. For many years in the past we closed our eyes to the Nazi threat. We must never allow ourselves to close them again. The danger to the world, to this country will not diminish. But it is possible to fight this danger if we know it, if we remain aware of its existence'. (Reiss, Curtis, The Nazis Go Underground. P201).

Bibliography

Baigent, Michael, *The Messianic Legacy*, Arrow Books, 1998

Baigent, Leigh and Lincoln, *The Holy Blood and the Holy Grail*, Arrow Books, 1969

Baigent, Michael & Leigh, Richard, *The Temple and the Lodge*, Arrow Books, 1998

Boudet, Abbe H, *The True Celtic Language and The Stone Circles of Rennes-les-Bains*, Les Editions De L, Oeil Du Sphinx, 2008 (from original of 1886)

Budge, Sir E. A. Wallis, KT, *The Book of the Cave of Treasures*, London Religious Tract Society, 1927

Buechner, Howard, *Emerald Cup - Ark of Gold*, Thunderbird Press, paperback, 1991.

Captier Antoine & Corbu Claire, *L'Heritage De L'Abbe Sauniere - Rennes-Le-Château*, Editions Belisane Cazilhac, 1985

Chaplin Patrice, *City of Secrets*, Constable & Robinson Ltd, 2007

Cicero, Chic & Cicero, Sandra, *The Essential Golden Dawn*, Llewellyn Publications, 2003

Donnelly, Ignatius, *Atlantis, the Antediluvian World*, Forgotten Books, 2007 (originally published 1882)

Fortune, Dion, *The Mystical Qabalah*, Weiser Books, 2000

Fanthorpe, Lionel & Patricia, *Mysteries of Templar Treasure & the Holy Grail – The Secrets of Rennes-Le-Chateau*, Weiser, 2004

Hatcher-Childress, David, *Pirates & The Lost Templar Fleet*, Adventures Unlimited Press, 2003

Hopkins, Marilyn, Simmans, Graham & Wallace-Murphy, Tim, *Rex Deus*, Element Books, 2000

Icke, David, *Alice in Wonderland & the World Trade Centre Disaster*, Bridge of Love Publications, 2002

Jung, Carl, Gustav, *The Archetypes And The Collective Unconscious, (The Collected Works of C. G. Jung, Vol. 9, Pt. 1)*, Princeton, 1969

Knight, Christopher & Lomas, Robert, *The Hiram Key*, Arrow Books, 1997

Knight, Christopher & Lomas, Robert, *Uriel's Machine*, Arrow Books, 2000

Levi, Eliphas, *Transcendental Magic*, Weiser, 1896 (first published 1896)

Lina, Juri, *Architects of Deception*, Referent Publishing, 2004

Lincoln, Henry, *The Holy Place*, Arcade Publishing, 1991

Lincoln, Henry, *Henry Lincoln's Guide to Rennes-le-Chateau and the Aude Valley (Video)*, Illuminated Word Ltd, 2002

Marrs, Jim, *The Rise of the Fourth Reich,* William Morrow, 2008

Martin, Sean, *The Cathars*, Pocket Essentials, 2005

Martin, Sean, *The Khights Templar*, Pocket Essentials, 2004

Mathers, MacGregor (translated), *The Key of Solomon the King*, George Redway, 1888

O'Shea, Stephen, *The Perfect Heresy – The Life and Death of the Cathars,* St. Edmundsbury Press, 2000

Picknett, Lynn & Prince, Clive, *The Templar Revelation*, Bantam Press, 1997

Putnam, Bill & Wood, Edwin, *The Treasure of Rennes-le-Chateau A Mystery Solved*, Sutton Publishing, 2003

Rahn, Otto, *Crusade Against the Grail*, Inner Traditions, 2006 (English translation)

Rahn, Otto, *Otto Rahn and the Quest for the Holy Grail: The Amazing Life of the Real "Indiana Jones"*, Adventures Unlimited Press, 2008

Rahn, Otto, *Lucifer's Court: A Heretic's Journey in Search of the Light Bringers*, Inner Traditions, 2008

Reiss, Curtis, *The Nazis Go Underground*, Doubleday, Doran and co, 1944

Regardie, Israel, *The Tree of Life*, Llewellyn Publications, 2002

Regardie, Israel, *The Golden Dawn: An Account of the Teachings, Rites and Ceremonies of the Order of the Golden Dawn*, Llewellyn Publications, 1986

Regardie, Israel, A Garden of Pomegranates, Llewellyn Publications, 1999

Robin, Jean-Luc, *Rennes-le-Chateau Sauniere's Secret*, Editions Sud Ouest,2007

de Sede, Gerard, *The Accursed Treasure of Rennes-le-Château*

de Sede, Gerard, *Rennes-le-Château*, DEK Publishing, 2006

Tsarion, Michael, *The Irish Origins of Civilisation – Vol 1*, Taroscopes, 2007

Tsarion, Michael, *The Irish Origins of Civilisation – Vol 2*, Taroscopes, 2007

Wallace-Murphy, Tim, *The Knights of the Holy Grail*, Watkins, 2007

Wier, Johann, *Pseudomonarchia daemonum* - (1583) (quoted)

Wolfram von Eschenbach, *Parzival*, Penguin Classics; Reprint edition, 2004

Wood, David, *Genisis: The First Book of Revelations*, Baton Press Ltd, 1985

Wood, David & Campbell, Ian, *Geneset: Target Earth*, Bellevue Books, 1994

The Cathar Country

Neil McDonald runs 'Megalithic Tours', to ancient, mystical and historical sites around Britain, France and Malta; from the famous Stonehenge, where we have private access, Callanish in the Outer Hebrides, Orkney and Shetland the amazing stone alignments of Carnac in Northern France etc; to many little known, hidden gems. The Megalithic Tours website contains an up to date timetable.

Cathar Country Tours
and Private Tours to the Cathar Country

Neil has been running comprehensive tours to the Cathar Country for some years and details can be found on the Megalithic Tours website. Private tours to the Cathar Country can also be arranged for groups of 4 or more people.

The Cathar Country

Megalithic Tours

50 Cottam Avenue
Ingol, Preston,
Lancashire
PR2 3XH. UK

01772 728181 – 07799 061991
neil@megalithictours.com

www.megalithictours.com

The Cathar Country